Let There Be Light

A Book for Encouragement, Character Building, and Kingdom Building

Lillian Colson Graham

ISBN 978-1-64416-662-8 (paperback)
ISBN 978-1-64416-663-5 (digital)

Copyright © 2019 by Lillian Colson Graham

All rights reserved. No part of this publication may be reproduced, distributed, or transmitted in any form or by any means, including photocopying, recording, or other electronic or mechanical methods without the prior written permission of the publisher. For permission requests, solicit the publisher via the address below.

Christian Faith Publishing, Inc.
832 Park Avenue
Meadville, PA 16335
www.christianfaithpublishing.com

Printed in the United States of America

Contents

Why?..5
Foreword..7
Discussion Topic #1: The Rising of the "Son" 13
Discussion Topic #2: First Things First 15
Discussion Topic #3: A View of Life 17
Discussion Topic #4: Wonder Working Power 19
Discussion Topic #5: Making a "You" Turn..............................21
Discussion Topic #6: Let the Past Be the Past..........................24
Discussion Topic #7: Teens and Parenting................................28
These Little Lights of Mine 36
    School Daze 36
    Let the Church Be a Light in Your Life...............................41
Poetic Lights to Live By 44
    Choose This Day...44
    Who Are You? 45
    Born Again..46
    God's Grace..47
    Reach Out...48
    The Gospel 50
    The Church 52
    Repentance...53
The Greatest of These is Love...56
The Greatest of These Is Love: A Tribute................................61
    Exhibit #1:   Congratulations to Mrs. Lillian Graham!........63
    Exhibit #2:   Just A Word!...64

Exhibit #3:	Valedictorian Speech and Some Wise Sayings from the Valedictorian Speech for Seniors to Be Guided By May 14, 1954	65
Exhibit #4:	Rapping for Jesus	68

The Value of Bible Knowledge 70
    Lights 70
    Son Lights (KJV) 70
    Search Lights (KJV) 72
    Bright Lights (KJV) 76
    Ceiling Lights (KJV) 79
    Dim Lights 81
    De-Lights 84
    Flashing Lights (KJV) 86
    Guiding Lights (KJV) 96
    Head Lights (KJV): 99
    Stop Lights 102
More Bible Knowledge 104
    Mountains Information 104
    Miracles (KJV) 105
    Parables 109
    The Twelve Tribes of Israel 112
    The Judges of Israel Years of Server 113
What Does the Bible Say About… (Holy Bible KJV) 114
Jesus's Disciples (12 Origin) (KJV) 117
How Many? 119
Thanks… 121
Benedictions 123

Why?

Ask me why I wrote this book, my answer.

* Because I need you to know that there are many ways to know and apply Bible knowledge.
* Because I need you to know that the Bible is not a dull book.
* Because I need you to know that if you look back over your life from birth until the present time, you will see that God was always there.
* Because I need you to know that God was not just there, he was there because you needed him throughout your whole life: because you are his child; because he knows your every need.
* I need you to know that we live in a world filled with sin. There will be ups and downs; good and some bad; some sick days and some sad days, some weeping days—but joy cometh in the morning.

I need you to know that God has provided us with things that will make life easier to bear. It reaches teachers, workshops, social media, books, DVDs—use them.

Foreword

Encouragement… For those who have not decided the road they will take, just keep on traveling, obey all the road signs and traffic lights, and read your road map.

Character Building… For those who have decided to travel, have decided which direction to travel, have read the directions and are ready to roll.

Kingdom…For those who are already traveling, ready to encourage others to travel, ready to actually help others along the way, and those who have said, Yes Lord!!!

LILLIAN COLSON GRAHAM

Aunt Christine Starling (Clowers) and
mother Elnora Horn (Clowers)

In the year of 1937:

* An average house cost about $4,250.00 the equivalent of $68,000.00 today.
* A typical new car cost about $800.00 or $12,800.00 in current dollars.
* The average annual wage was about $1,000.00 which equates to $16,000.00 today.
* At an average cost of 23 cents per movie ticket (more than $3.00 in today's money), the movies were still a favorite way to escape from harsh economic realities …

* Grocery-store prices:

    – White bread, one loaf: 8 cents
    – Milk, one gallon: 50 cents
    – Sugar, one pound: 5 cents
    – Eggs, one dozen: 18 cents
    – Bacon, one pound: 38 cents
    – Peanut butter, one quart: 23 cents
    – Corn flakes, one box: 7 cents
    – Ketchup, one bottle: 9 cents
    – Wieners, one pound: 8 cents
    – Chicken, one pound: 20 cents
    – Hamburger meat, one pound: 12 cents
    – Steak, one pound: 22 cents
    – Catfish, one pound: 28 cents
    – Pork and beans, one can: 5 cents

- Tomato soup, four cans: 25 cents
- Potatoes, one pound: 2 cents
- Lettuce, one head: 7 cents
- Peas, one pound: 4 cents

* Personal-care items:

  - Toothpaste: 30 cents
  - Talcum powder: 13 cents
  - Toilet tissue, two rolls: 9 cents

* Beverages and side orders:
  - Coca-Cola: 5 cents
  - Milk, tea, hot chocolate, or pot of coffee: 10 cents
  - French-fried or julienne potatoes: 20 cents
  - Toast: dry, 10 cents; buttered, 15 cents

* Children's toys price:

  - Baby doll that cries, sleeps, drinks and wets: 69 cents
  - Tricycle: $4.69
  - Lionel train set, with switches and tracks: $9.95
  - Parcheesi game: 89 cents

* Luxury items:

  - 5-lb. box of chocolates: $1.98
  - Ladies' watch, chrome finish: $5.95
  - Men's 10K gold ring with initial: $4.98

Information taken from:
The Year in History 1937
Whitman Publishing LLC 2012
pp. 15, 17, 19

Some people refuse to believe what they call bad luck is just darkness that they refuse to conquer. There are times when we all need to look up, reach up, and stand up! And see the light of course "into" each life some rain will fall, but remember God's light is eternal and behind the clouds, the sun is still shining. This is to say that God's light is eternal and there for us all from birth throughout life.

However, he provides through many sources.

Ask questions, make a "U" turn, read books, watch movies, study, seek educational sources.

Never become a know-it-all (unteachable); pull a string, flick a switch, turn a knob, try a different way. We know we walk in darkness when we can't find our way, when we reach and feel no support, when we call and get no answer, when we stumble and sometimes fall. Call on the Almighty Father who is always there (prayer). Read, study, and understand scripture (Bible study), take a look at your past sometime. Your lesson is behind you (Past experience can teach valuable lessons), and search yourself. For your hidden ignored talents can light the pathway for others (singing, teaching, reaching, writing, smooth talking).

Go forth, look for light, it's there!

Amen.

Twelve years ago, I lost my sight, and five years ago, I lost part of my hearing. I don't want any pity and I have no desire to question God, we live in a sinful world and sometimes things happen. I was able to see and do so many things before I lost my vision, and still do what I can to enlarge God's Kingdom. What I'm saying is whatever is in God's will for me is also my will. I thank God for allowing me to watch my two sons grow into strong men. Also, I'm so thankful for my ten grandchildren as they mature and begin on their journey in life.

"Let thy will be done."

Discussion Topic # 1
The Rising of the "Son"

The birth, teachings, death, and resurrection of Jesus Christ serves to transform our lives. Jesus was dishonored often, but not because he went about doing good or performing miracles, or speaking in parables. He would have been considered a compassionate miracle worker. It was his teaching that got his enemies against him. His teaching caused them to take their complaint to the Roman officials. Those same teachings are still stirring people up today, why? Because they continue to challenge to change their lifestyles and practices, they consider it impossible to live like Jesus.

Forgiveness

One difficult area would be forgiveness. It is one thing to read about Jesus and his willingness to forgive but it is quite another thing to actually forgive. We are to forgive others just as Christ has forgiveness. Forgiveness is probably the toughest test in this Christian journey. At the same time, it is one of the most beautiful expressions of our love for one another. It expresses an attitude of reconciliation.

Compassion

Our society has taught us to be comfortable in "walking on the other side" when we see others in distress, especially if that person is not in our circle. Jesus's teachings challenges us to become sensitive to the needs of others and to become active in helping to meet those needs, even when it will cost us. When Jesus came and met our needs, it cost him his life. The parable of the Good Samaritan teaches us who our neighbors really are and our responsibility to them. It teaches us that God is not impressed with status, even a headful of religious facts will not make up for the lack of compassion. Christianity is not in the brain. It is in the heart; not in the church building but in the community where people are in need of salvation.

Light Beam #1: The Rising of the "Son"
Questions:

1. Why did Jesus come to Earth?
2. Why did Jesus stay on Earth the length of time he did?
3. What is the difference between righteousness and grace?
4. If Jesus had not died on the cross, what would have been mankind's destiny?
5. What does it mean when we say "sin nature?"

Discussion Topic # 2
First Things First

Life on the earth is preparation for life beyond the life we spend here. Everything we do should help us get ready for life beyond. However, we sometimes do foolish things, it is possible that many times we are giving up what we should hold on to, and holding on to what we should give up. Sometimes, we gain worldly things, but give up our souls. When we do this, we are deceiving ourselves. It is not wise to major in minors. How are we to prepare our souls for that final day? One way is to live a life where we acknowledged Jesus as Lord before man. If we do this, he will acknowledge us before God. Jesus made it clear that the treatment God gives us on that day will be determined by the priority we give to him and his son while on this earth. Some of the most common priorities that Christians must set for themselves are:

1. Prayer, study, and worship.
2. Concern for our image before others.
3. Concern for our physical body which God has given us.
4. Concern for material blessings.
5. Our use of time, which is all provided by God.

Here are some questions that will help us to evaluate ourselves in putting "First Things, First":

1. What do you do first when the company gives you a raise?
2. What are your first thoughts of what you would do if you suddenly became wealthy?

3. What is the first thing you do when you wake in the morning?
4. How often do you read/study the word of God?
5. What do you do when you see a person is in need (even if you don't know them)?
6. What is your reaction to stewardship campaigns in church?
7. What is your reaction to campaigns to help charity organizations?

There is nothing wrong with being richly blessed, there is nothing wrong with living a comfortable life, there is nothing wrong with being able to afford an education for our children. There is something wrong with being selfish, there is something wrong with being greedy, there is something wrong with not offering service to others.

Light Beam #2: First Things First
Questions:

1. What is the first thing you do when you wake up in the morning? Why?
2. What is the last thing you do before you go to bed at night? Why?
3. What are some of the consequences for doing things out of order?
4. What order did God create the Earth?
5. What would have been the consequences if God created man before he created lights?

Discussion Topic # 3
A View of Life

What is your view of your life? Do you view your life as being orderly? Does it make sense or is it marked by utter confusion? Do you see merely a human tangle or can you discern a divine plan? Do you see life as a set part of a giant universe? Do you view your life as being wound-up and left to run on its own? Do you view your life as empty and meaningless?

When we diagnose our world and we find our rightful place in it, we see much anguish and alienation. Personal and social problems have never been greater; depression is causing emotional disorder; so many people feel hopeless. Humans have found escape solutions such as drugs, alcohol, gambling, shopping sprees, and sexual adventures. This is the mood of a people that concentrate on immediate gratification and self fulfillment. I am reminded of the biblical description of a pagan world that is "without God and without hope" to them, life seems to be made up by chance of accident and by uncontrolled circumstances.

The best cure for this kind of life is found in the word of God. There are the stories of a God who cares and who creates and who involves himself in the lives of his people. He offers us a new and different view of life. God promised that through Abraham, all the families of the earth would be blessed ... through biblical _____? God proved himself to be faithful and trustworthy.

God does not will mankind to do evil. Evil comes through the living will of those who rebel against God. He permits afflictions, trials, anguish, and tribulations. He permits many conditions that he does not cause. God's blessings can bring us out of our troubles.

Light Beam #3: A View of Life
Questions:

1. What part of your life would you say was (or is) most enjoyable?
2. Do you feel that you deserve everything that happened to you in your life? Why or why not?
3. If you were asked to define "life," what would you say?
4. What would you say is a successful life?
5. Do you believe in life after death?

Discussion Topic # 4
Wonder Working Power

Our Father who art in heaven, I know you are the creator and controller of all things. I believe your "will" is for my good. Help me to see beyond selfish or short-term gain and put your "will" above any wish of mine. Help me to serve you and others truly sincerely.

>Father I pray that You will be my
>GOD in all things and that You will
>Order my steps along the way; that
>You will increase my territory as
>I increase in You; that You will
>Open my heart so that I will
>Appreciate every blessing coming from you!
>In JESUS name
>For Thine is the Kingdom and
>The power and the Glory

And lead us not into temptation, but deliver us from evil: For thine is the kingdom, and the power, and the glory, forever. Amen.
(Matthew 6:13)

And His power shall be mighty, but not by His own power ...
(Daniel 8:24)

Let every soul be subject to the higher powers, for there is no higher power, except the powers that be ordained of GOD.

(Romans 13:1)

Light Beam #4: Wonder Working Power
Questions:

1. How would you describe the word "respect?"
2. What does it mean to "love your enemy?"
3. "To love God," to love your neighbor, to love your children, to love your enemy, what is the likeness in all and what are the differences in all?
4. Define the word love?
5. Define the word godliness?
6. Which one needs more work in your life?

Discussion Topics # 5
Making a "You" Turn

In this life, as we travel down the life highway we need to turn around—make a "you turn." Sometimes, the road used to travel is filled with envy, jealousy, hatred, disrespect, ungodly habits, addictions, crime, gossip, backbiting, homicide, suicide, robbery, sex perversion, lying, idol worship, pedophilia, and fear. We wonder where we made a wrong turn and got off the road of love, humility, patience, long suffering, perseverance, godliness, faithfulness, obedience – all attributes that please God and assure our relationship with God. You have time to make a "you turn." You have time to turn jealousy into joy; hatred into humility, murmuring into mission. Just remember on life's highway you will encounter several types of people, there will be other believers, non-believers, there will be those who have made "you turns," those who need to make the turn, those who need help in order, to make the turn, there will be those who will need professional help in order to change directions. My point being whatever situation you find yourselves in, you are not alone. It is time to change, it is necessary to change.

The word of God is your recipe for change. It encourages, demands, and assists in the change. Remember you are not alone. Believers must also "let the past be the past: and focus on the present. I say this because we all have baggage that will continue to slow our travel if we don't leave it behind. Today, we can learn true praise and worship, attend Bible study, attend church services, join Evangelism and witness groups; learn to discern; remain teachable; increase your prayer life; walk the walk; talk the talk; and live the life.

"If my people who are called by My Name shall humble themselves, and pray and seek my face and turn from their wicked ways then will I hear from Heaven and will forgive their sins and will heal their land."
(2 Chronicles 7:14 KJV)

For I know that in me (that is, in my flesh,) dwelleth no good thing: for to will is present with me; but how to perform that which is good I find not. But I see another law in my members, warring against the law of my mind, and bringing me into captivity to the law of sin which is in my members. O wretched man that I am! who shall deliver me from the body of this death? I thank God through Jesus Christ our Lord. So then with the mind I myself serve* the law of God; but with the flesh the law of sin.

Thank GOD it has been done by JESUS Christ our LORD He has set me free.
(Romans 7:18, 23–25 KJV)

"Brethren, I count not myself to have apprehended: but this one thing I do, forgetting those things which are behind, and reaching forth unto those things which are before, I press toward the mark for the prize of the high calling of God in Christ Jesus."
(Philippians 3:13–14 KJV)

Light Beam #5: Making a "You" Turn
Questions:

1. What are some wrong turns in life and some you would need to turn around?
2. What are some wrong exits in life?
3. What are some "slow down" signs?
4. What are some "change lanes" signs?
5. If you found yourself on the wrong road, what would you do?

Mother (Elnora) and niece (Tiffany) visiting the cotton fields in Georgia

Discussion Topic #6
Let the Past Be the Past

Do you ever wonder why the slaves were brought to America? Do you wonder why the race has undergone so much suffering? Do you wonder why others of various national origins seem to prosper while the Black Americans seem to stand still? Do you understand why Black Americans are plagued with hatred, bigotry, prejudices, abuse, and discrimination?

Answers to these questions are not easy to come by. Therefore, we as a race must look three ways where we were, where we are, and where we can be, knowing that we can do all things through Christ who strengthen us. We were helpless but not hopeless; we were stomped but not stopped; we were beat but not bent; we were shut out, but not snuffed out; during the late forties and the early fifties, I was a youngster growing up in my hometown. I would like to shake some of the horrors I experienced and witnessed. Surrounding my hometown were cotton plantations and tobacco farms. I picked cotton because that was what we considered summer jobs now. The tobacco experience was quite different. Many kids would go to the tobacco farms to work. Well, I decided to try that. My adopted stepmother and father gave me permission to do so. However, I did notice the smiles they both had on their faces. I worked and to my horror, there were worms there that were the size of a very large cigar. They were green with two bulging eyes and two horns. Needless to say, I freaked out. I completely lost it because I was and had always been deathly afraid of worms. Psalms 55:1: *Give ear to my prayer, O GOD, and hide not Thyself from my supplications.* I was brought back home about midday. Those smiles on my parents' faces had turned to pure laughter. That was the end of the tobacco career.

"Segregation, Before Laws Were Passed and Enforced"

White people only lived in the Northern part of town and colored people lived in the Southern section of town, outside of City limits. The Northern section of town had paved streets, street lights, sewer service, and door-to-door mail service. The Southern section of town had dirt roads, no street lights, no sewer service (cesspools if anything), and no door-to-door mail service. "Colored" people were allowed to purchase groceries on credit but when they were not able to pay for groceries or pay their rent collectors, they were mysteriously taken from their families and beaten. Restaurants, water fountains, public bathrooms, cabs, voting polls, bus and train transportation, movies (colored people in the balcony and white people downstairs), sports arenas, schools, colleges, and churches were separate. But, "God is no respector of persons…A tornado came through town one day, jumped over the Southern portion of town and did some very destructive damage to the Northern portion. Guess who were asked to come and help rebuild?

Another incident occurred in Atlanta, where I attended college during the time when the first African-American male student was admitted to the University of Georgia as a student. While on a shopping pass to downtown Atlanta, we came face-to-face with a parade of Ku-Klux-Klan members. We were not approached but we didn't need to be. I had heard plenty about the Klan, but had never seen them. The Klu Klux Klan made regular Klan garbed showings and burned crosses even after the segregation laws were passed. My parents in Connecticut got a big kick when I wrote and told them that "The Klan was walking the streets just like real people." I don't want to make it all sound bad. A famous Jazz band leader, Duke Ellington and his band passed through my hometown (Tifton) heading North from a Florida tour, he had a serious accident. The band leader was hospitalized and placed in the "colored" section of the hospital. Oh Boy! He promised to return and sponsor a dance; in the airport hanger for whites and blacks together and donate the proceeds to the hospital and build an addition for an integrated wing to the hospital. All was done. All was happy long before the segregation laws were passed in 1954.

Now that we have seen a blast from the past, Let's take a look at the Nation today. The picture is not beautiful, but it is nowhere as "ugly" as it has been – the more reason we must "let the past be the past." We are faced with social injustices, drug and alcohol addictions; child abuse; molestation; hatred; prejudices; job promotion and placement, discrimination; property ownership discrimination; credit bias, and other lingering effects of slavery and the post slavery period.

However, presently, our generations can see African-American business owners, state and Nation politicians, teachers and administrators of integrated educational institutions, radio, newspaper, television personalities, governors, and mayors, firemen and police officers, realtors and construction company owners; millionaires, supermodels, actors and actress; great comedians, doctors, lawyers, and judges, corporation executives; bookkeepers and accountants; students at any college or university. Being permitted to sit in any available seat on public transportation; being able to be served in any restaurant; being safe to fight for any injustice; and we can see an African-American president (two terms) of these United States of America. Who knows what's in the future. We must drive forward and see.

Let the Past Be the Past

Question:

> If you were rescued from a well of water,
> even if you are still wet from water
> would you want to go back into the well?

> *I can do all things through Christ which strengthen me.* (Philippians 4:3)

Light Beam #6: Let the Past Be the Past
Questions:

1. What good things do you remember about your past?
2. What bad things do you remember about your past?
3. What lessons do you remember from your past?
4. Where did you get the strength to get over the negative things of the past?
5. Would you want to forget the past? Why? Why not?

Discussion Topic #7
Teens and Parenting

The question is:

Are the church* programs sufficiently planned to bash boredom, open minds, reach hearts, teach values, introduce righteous standards? When I was a teen some decades ago, there was hardly any trouble to get into. If you dared to try smoking cigarettes, some neighbor would see you and report it to your parents. If you went to a sports game, your parents took you. If you went to a party or a school dance, your parents were there. Drugs had not been fully introduce. Alcohol was illegal since the county was a "dry county." No one owned a computer yet. There was one television (black and white—no cable) in the neighborhood which was in the home of a school teacher. Entertainment was Hopscotch, Dodgeball, Hide-and-seek, Old Maid cards, Pick-up-sticks, Tom Walker's, bike riding, Sunday picnics, visits to grandmother's for homemade ice cream, and night time story telling. There were no fast food restaurants. However, there were Saturday night fish frys. There were very few job opportunities for teens except farm work. If you lived in town, you could be transported to the farm daily to work in picking cotton, cropping tobacco, and shaking peanuts. The celebrations included Christmas (gifts, food, school vacation), Easter (eggs and pageants), sports (Football, Basketball), and homecoming game. There were summer camps (NHA—New Homemakers of America) for the girls and NFA was for the boys (New Farmers of America). This was not fun since it was in very rural areas where there was an oversupply of wild animals, If you didn't see them by day, you certainly heard them howl by night. Naturally, I didn't last long at camp before I had to be taken to the corner store (no cell phones) to call my parents to be returned home. The family car was standard shift.

However, we could drive at very early ages since no one cared. Everyone wanted to finish high school and go to college, which was an escape from the small town. Many boys escaped to the Armed Forces. During World War I, certain foods and products were "rationed" (limited). Families were issued stamps to allow them to purchase limited supplies. Most families raised chickens and pigs and planted gardens. Minority businesses were: beauty parlors, building, cafe's, Juke joints, cleaners, small grocery stores, funeral parlors, domestic cleaning, cab drivers, school teachers (segregated schools). Segregated places: hospitals, schools, restaurants, water fountains in stores, public transportation, communities, churches, doctors, dentist offices and voting facilities. Unmarried couples living together were unheard of. Spousal abuse was common (No women's Lib), child abuse was common (No CPS), poverty was common (No Welfare). Robbery, murder, suicide were rare happenings since the people in the communities cared deeply for each other. The above information is shared in order to give the reader a view from the past.

I am sure some life experiences of others were better and some were worse. However, by sharing those experiences it enables me to jump to the present times facing today's youth. Some of the tragic things facing them: peer pressure, drug addiction, alcoholism, Internet entanglement, child abuse, child molestation, broken and unstable homes, date rape, teen pregnancy, gang violence, prostitution enticement, violence and sex on TV, violence and sex in music, violence and sex in movies, violence and sex in magazines, shoplifting enticement, anti-spiritual attitudes, disrespect for authority, lack of homemaking skills, lack of listening skills, lack of proper communication skills, texting and Facebook has replaced proper English, dwindling reading, writing, spelling skills. I take this moment to applaud the teens who are determined to be upright godly members of this society. Keep up the good work!

However, our teens are facing abuse in several areas: physical, verbal, emotional, and sexual. Therefore, many teens have become crippled emotionally. Our churches and communities must be equipped with youth workers that are sensitive, supportive, resourceful, diligent, teachable, and committed. They must be aware of the teen problems of the present times. Therefore, their skills must be constantly updated. Their knowledge has to be increased and applied. They must know how to gain the trust of the young people. Many teens are angry and resentful, depressed, and misguided. Therefore the workers must be professionally trained by education or experience. They must be willing and able to work with groups and individuals since the teen problems can be so varied. They must be prepared to address problems and situations that arise in the family and out of the family.

The questions the churches and communities must ask themselves about their youth workers:

1.) Are they experienced workers?
2.) Are they sympathetic to the problems of the present-time teen?
3.) Are they supportive of young people?
4.) Do they practice confidentiality?
5.) Are they capable of dispelling anger, resentment, disrespect, depression, dishonesty?
6.) Can the youth worker remain neutral in all situations, except applying knowledge between good and evil?
7.) Are the workers aware of and in touch with appropriate resources?
8.) Does the lifestyle of the worker reflect the values they teach?
9.) Do they believe in God?

"Let all bitterness, and wrath, and anger, and clamour, and evil speaking, be away from you, with all malice: And be ye kind one to another, even as God for Christ's sake hath forgiven you." Ephesians 4:31–32 (KJV)

My point is that our teens are smart, therefore the youth leaders must be smart. Our teens are streetwise, therefore our youth leaders must be spiritual-wise. Our teens must be taught that the back burner is no place for God's word.

Teach them that salvation comes only through Jesus Christ and the work he did on the cross. Teach them about prayer, Bible study, the effects of sin, teach them about praise and worship. Teach them the effects of pride; teach them about God's grace and mercy; teach them that God calls the young as well as the elderly from death to life. In order to teach these things, the youth leaders must possess what they confess. They must be guided by the Holy Spirit and they possess a god-given vision—all these things through prayer, diligence, humility, and commitment, and study.

> *Young woman, young man there will be a helping hand*
> *Your lives are filled with things to do*
> *But, are these things to benefit you*
> *Your lives are filled with places to go*
> *When you sense trouble, just say no!*
> *Your lives are filled with many choices*
> *You will hear so many voices*
> *Remember a helping hand is there*
> *Reach-out- Grab-hold*
> *Hold on-Take care*
> *Helping hands: Preachers, Teachers, Christians,*
> *Community workers, Youth Workers, Professionals in the field.*

> *Humble yourselves under the mighty Hand of God that He may exalt you in due time.*
> *"Casting all your cares upon Him; for He careth for you. Be sober, be vigilant because your adversary, the devil, as a roaring lion, walketh about, seeking whom he may devour."* 1 Peter 5:6–8 (KJV)

Save Our Teens/Parenting:

Parenting is not easy anymore, parenting is not like it was before.

May I, please, and thank you, have gone right out of the door society is teaching what they need to know.

The clothes are too short, too tight, and too bare. Manners went out of the window with respect. Parents, if you have teens who heed to your teaching keep on praying, teaching and reaching. It takes love, tears, punishment, but we all must know that kids today are facing many dangers that were never foreseen. To mention—drugs (selling and using), prostitution-girls and boys, rape-girls and boys-babies and little children, sex slaves girls and boys, social media, dates, children killing parents, parents killing children, and the list goes on. Why are parents remaining the same when the generations are changing so much? Are the teens wiser than the parents? Do the parents even know how to change?

Questions for Group Discussion—Self-Examination/ Conversation:

1. Why don't teens like to attend church?
2. Why is it that the teens today seem to be going wild?
3. What is your definition of respect?
4. What does it mean to honor your mother and father? (What if you think they are wrong)

Biological Mother and Father (Elnora Horn and McKinley Mays)

Father – McKinley Mays

Adoptive mother, Minnie Colson, known as Madear (mother dear)

Adoptive father, Norman Colson

Allen Temple (recent picture), the church
Lillian attended as a young girl

These Little Lights of Mine

School Daze

I am Lillian Leola Graham born in Adel, Georgia to McKinley Mays and Mary Elnora Clowers, April 1, 1937. My father lived in Adel, and was a very popular fellow. He had other children that I knew from a distance (McKinley, Jr. [Sonny], James Wesley [Poppa], Maxie B., and Ann). I was his oldest child. My mother had another daughter (Arlene).

Now that all the lights are on I can remember early years of moving to Hatley, Georgia, near Cordele, Georgia with my mother. Many older relatives have told me many times that I was too young to remember those years. But they were wrong I remember living in Hatley, Georgia. I remember the Peacock Family, (the only family with a white house), the Starling Family (whose house was near the train track, you would visit them in order to see the train) the Cross Family, (who never invited you inside the house), the John Brown Family, who gave me my first pet chicken (a frizzly hen). I remember the rolling store that would come through one (1) day a week.

After returning to Adel, Georgia, grades kindergarten through fourth (I was skipped from first to third grade), were spent with my great-grandmother until age eight, who was the towns midwife and delivered most babies in town (black and white). I was adopted by my mother's cousin Minnie Lee Lilly Colson and her husband Norman Lee Colson, whom I knew as "mother dear" and "daddy". In the year 1945, daddy returned from World War II and I was taken to live in Tifton, Georgia. I was now Lillian Leola Colson. This was my family who provided very well for me.

Grades four to nine, the only remembrance I have here is that in grade nine, I went to school half days because there was no room in the school for "grammar" classes.

Therefore, I was taught for a half day and at the age of fourteen, I taught second grade in the afternoon class. (there was one school for all grades).

The reason for this is the black men in the neighborhood who worked for the Armour Meat Co., went on strike and were not financially prepared to strike therefore they crossed the picket line.

This resulted in all their homes being bombed. The principal of the school asked the teachers and students to bring food and clothing for the families of the victims, which resulted in the school being bombed. Army barracks were brought to the school site for classroom use, until a new school was constructed.

This was not sufficient for all day school so there were morning and evening sessions, (school was for all ages). Because of this, there was a shortage of teachers and the high school students were used to help teach the younger students (I taught the second grade), this lasted for approximately three months.

School days at home were to be remembered after all, they are the reason I am who I am.

From a very small child, I attended the Allen Temple AME Church. Monday through Friday were school days unless you were ill; and if you were ill, you stayed home (in bed) until you gotten well again. Our area in the United States was known to be hit by tornadoes. School was so important that we were taught should we get caught in a tornado: get in a ditch, lie face down and stay there until the tornado passed over. Then return home, change into clean and dry clothes and return to school. In other words, there was no such thing as "no school days." I wasn't even that lucky because I lived across the football field from the school. So I could remain home until the storm passed by. At the end of the week was Saturday which was "chore" day. The cleaning, the washing, the repairs, the yard work, the cooking for Sunday, and the shopping. Now comes Sunday and special holidays which were special in the eyes of all! Sunday was a day of rest, worship, praise, thanksgiving, ministry, and good works. The work and repairs were done by the men and boys of the church before Sunday and other inside preparations were done by the women and girls. Sunday School began promptly at 9:00 a.m. and ended at 11:00 a.m. The whole family attended both of course, we kids could go to the community soda fountain between services. But "you better be back here in fifteen minutes," said mother. After morning worship, we went home to Sunday dinner which could include chicken, stuffing, squash, turnip greens, candied yams, pot roast, corn bread, and banana pudding, caramel cake, or peach cobbler for dessert. After dinner and a short rest period, it was back to church for the afternoon service at 5:00 p.m. which lasted anywhere from two to three hours.

These were the fun years. Tenth, eleventh and twelfth grades, Oh Boy! Were filled with drama and spelling competitions by school districts and regionals (bragging because I won first place medals on all levels in dramatics). The girls joined the New Homemakers of America (NHA) club and were taught to cook and sew. The boys joined the New Farmers of America (NFA) where they were taught to raise and tend animals and chickens and grow gardens.

They had their own farm land which was loaned to them. We joined the school glee club (choir) and sang for schools and community affairs. I was a part of an all-girls singing group called "La Cheerios" where we sang at proms and weddings throughout southern Georgia.

One bright memory is that of a nightclub experience, there was a provision for service men who went into the military before they finished high school when they returned home and enrolled in school they were provided government support until they graduated. We had two of those guys in our senior class. One guy bought a nightclub with his allotment; and that's where a few of us spent our lunch time dancing and having fun. Then one day, I decided to do like the others and drink a beer just as I took my first mouthful, someone yelled, "Here comes the principal." Well, that one mouthfull of beer went up and came out of my nose. Psalms 139:23-24: *"Search me, O GOD, and know my heart; try me and know my anxieties; and see if there is any wicked way in me, and lead me in the way everlasting."* That was my first and only taste of beer. (Of course the principal was not coming).

Then…

There was the time when five of us girls and boys took the NFA truck, went downtown and into court to listen to the lawyers present their cases. When court was over, we returned to where we had parked. Holy smoke! The truck was not there, it had been towed. Towed for illegal parking, there we were with no money to get the truck and no way to get back to the school, where we were in no hurry to go. Psalms 63:1 (KJV): *"O God, You are my God; I seek You; my soul thirsts for You; my soul longs for you as in a dry and weary land where there is no water."* However, we thought of the dad of one of the boys, his dad owned a cleaners at the edge of town, we went there and he got the truck for us. But, to repay him, we had to report to him after school every day for a week and deliver cloths by foot in the hot Georgia sun. We got no sympathy from our parents. Even when we had to stay after school for another week.

Well…

There was the time when the eighth graders were angry at the ninth graders. We decided to fight it out. We decided to meet at the centerline of the football field. The eighth graders on the Southside and ninth graders on the Northside. I don't remember who, but someone pushed someone and—oh boy—it was on then. You guessed it, another week of punishment. However, after the fight, the two grades were friends again.

Also…

There was the apple episode. Every year, the county officials would send crates of big red, juicy apples to the school. The teacher would take as many as she wanted out of the crate brought to our classroom, and the class could have what was left. One day, the apples came and the teacher was not in the room. Well we ate them all. She was so angry and after she had told us off she went and got the principal. Psalms 46:1: *"God is our Refuge and Strength, a very present help in trouble."* Well, he was angry too. We had to stay in school until six o'clock and eat apples all that time. One crate after another. We tried to be sick, but sick wouldn't come, and again the parents laughed. I think they laughed all of our high school years.

I am also reminded of the time the whole class was under punishment. There was an out-of-town football game, one class member was on the team, and the bus was loaded with the team members ready to go, but he was being detained in class. The teacher left the classroom for some reason. The boys in the class lifted him out of the window and he left with the team. We were asked one-by one where was the player, no one answered. This amounted to three hours after school detention, no walking, talking, or sleeping.

One more…

Our Science Teacher decided to take our class on a field trip into the woods to catch snakes for a science project (Hot Doggity). We were equipped with a pronged stick and a burlap bag (which was called a croaker sack). We were instructed to catch the snake's head between the prongs, grab the snake by the tail, and throw him into the bag (okay, got it). Off into the woods we went. After searching for about an hour the boys yelled "we found one!". The teacher led the way running out of the woods followed by the whole class. Naturally there was no snake. That was the end of our hands-on reptile education.

There are many more good and funny times however time nor paper will allow.

Then…

It was graduation time. Graduation was held in the movie theater. The principal and teachers marched in first, wearing their robes and collars that told what degree they had earned. Then came our class. Not bragging, but I was the valedictorian of the class and had to learn a very long speech. (See Exhibit # 3 A Valedictorian Speech)

The principal gave a beautiful speech. I can remember some of his powerful words. "I am so glad to get rid of this class. It is the worst class that I can remember,- The only class I don't want to remember." Psalms 47:1: *"Clap your hands, all ye peoples! Shout to God with loud songs of Joy!"* Then some of us went to college, some went into the military, some went to work, some just went.

Finally...

I said this to say, our past "Lights" the way to our future. Let the church be the center of your life. Praise, worship, prayer, and thanksgiving are necessary to light your way.

I have shared my life story with you because everybody has a past. Your past should not determine your future, but it provides little building blocks and little illuminated pathways to the future.

Let the Church Be a Light in Your Life

From my childhood experience, I still remember some words from the hymns and spirituals: "Just As I Am" (My favorite), "Amazing Grace," "The Church's One Foundation," "Holy, Holy," (the choir always marched in by) "Jesus is All the World to Me," "Yes God is Real," "Christ Is All," "There Is a Fountain," "He Arose," "Christ the Lord Is Risen Today," "Silent Night," "The First Noel," (many more Christmas), "If It Had Not Been for the Lord on My Side," "Precious Memories," "Humble Me," just to name a few.

Thanksgiving was a day of cooking, eating turkey, rabbit, squirrel, opossum, or raccoon that the man next door hunted, caught, cleaned cooked, and brought over to add to our dinner. "That was sickening to me because we never ate that." Thanksgiving a time to thank God for all blessings. One story, I'll share with you my little cousin (Billy) came to spend the thanksgiving week with us. The neighbor brought a whole cooked squirrel over. He entered the kitchen through the back door (nobody knocked during those days), he plopped this animal in the middle of our Sunday dinner. Naturally, everyone almost choked. However, my little cousin thought he would save the day. He said, "Would someone please pass me a piece of that rat?" Naturally, everyone left the table in a hurry.

Christmas: A real joyful time. A time for our neighbors and friends to visit, a time to cook and share favorite cooking, a time to share and show love for our friends and love ones. A time to show love just as GOD showed His love for us when He sent JESUS Christ to earth. To show our love to GOD, we spent time in Midday service on Christmas day. Then back home to open gifts and spend time with friends and loved ones. On the Sunday before or after Christmas, the Christmas program was presented with speeches, and skits and teens presented speeches, readings and pageants. The celebration was in the place of the evening service. I can remember saying a Christmas and Easter speech plus I had to learn a long part in the Christmas play. Other kids could not laugh because they had to do the same: children and teens whose family did not require them to participate in the church's program were considered to be non-Christian.

I love thy Church O' Lord Her walls before me stand ...

Easter was a time for sadness followed by joy. Sadness was preached on Good Friday.

The whole church was adorned with blossoming honeysuckle and its beautiful strong fragrance filled the church. Jesus praying in the garden: "*These words spake Jesus, and lifted up his eyes to heaven, and said, Father, the hour is come; glorify thy Son, that thy Son also may glorify thee: As thou hast given him power over all flesh, that he should give eternal life to as many as thou hast given him. And this is life eternal, that they might know thee the only true God, and Jesus Christ, whom thou hast sent. I have glorified thee on the earth: I have finished the work which thou gavest me to do.*" (John 17:1–4) In the service, the preacher spoke on the life of Jesus Christ, his message to the world, his purpose on the earth, and his promises. (All of which I had to be able to talk about once I got home. To prove that I was listening).

Sunday commemorating, Christ's resurrection from the dead Christ's victory over sin and death, and he gained eternal life for mankind—again I had to be able to talk about it.)

My message is, "Praise The Creator not the creation."

Poetic Lights to Live By
Choose This Day

As we study the scriptures, we become convinced that access to God's salvation is a matter of choice; choice to live a righteous life; choice to read and heed the word of God; choice to love and appreciate Jesus Christ for the work he did on the cross. Once we have made such choices, we must spend the rest of our lives moving toward sanctification; moving toward the perfection of our relationship with God. After we make the choice, we can make a deliberate attempt to live holy with assistance of the Holy Spirit, our inner devotion and dedication will activate God's grace and mercy. Then we begin to grow and mature. We begin to create ways to exercise our faith. We begin to encourage others to live holy. We begin to perform acts of justice and mercy. We begin to lead people to repentance. We are to live in love and holiness—then we will grow and grow, and grow spiritually. Now we come in full knowledge of justification knowing that it is only by the grace of God through Jesus Christ. Knowing that it is not dependent upon any human act or achievement. Now we come in full knowledge of sanctification. Sanctification being a cooperation between God and the Christian. When "The Saints Go Marching In," they will be a product of this partnership. These saints will have done their part in taming the flesh and cultivating the spirit.

> *"Choose ye this day whom ye will serve." (Joshua 24:15)*

Who Are You?

Prayer, Worship, Study, Praise the Works to God's Amazing Grace
Charity, Humility, Sacrifice, Intersessional Service, Compassion, Faith and Confession
Steadfast, Bold, Truthful, and Loyal
Rooted, Controlled, Empathetic and Joyful
Obedience, Belief, Respect for the Word
The Role of the Sheep, since Christ is the Shepherd.
The past is the past, leave it behind
Enjoying God's gift of a peaceful mind
Lying, Cheating, Stealing - All goes away
No Adultery, Fornication - This is your new day
Love your neighbor without consideration
For Race, Color, Creed, and other Nations
Put your trust in Jesus, He'll hear your call
He's the same Master that walked through the wall.
Patience, Justice, Works and Diligence
Always Exhibiting Spiritual intelligence
Drug Addiction, Alcoholism, Gambling needs Spiritual and Social Help.
God Almighty provides it sometimes step by step
Welcome to the Christian Life-

                Lillian Colson Graham 2015

Born Again

Newly renewed, Spiritual Birth committing to God who created the earth.
Bowing down to the Father, the Spirit and Son.
Acknowledging the Trinity is God, three and one
Setting priorities in accordance with God's will
Knowing that His promises will be fulfilled.
A right relationship with God is a born again goal
Then approaching God's throne confident and bold
You have now reached a level that is Holy and new
You have now reached a level where God can use you
Spiritual boldness you have reached
The level of Spiritual wholeness
You Are Born Again!

                Lillian Colson Graham 2015

God's Grace

Favor from our God Almighty above
Favor from our God so filled with Love,
Unending favor just for mankind
A gift from God for Mind, Body, and Soul
A gift from God of Eternal Life
That Gift comes only through belief in Jesus Christ.
A gift from above that we do not deserve
Don't take for granted in our failure to serve.
Be thankful, be grateful, be filled with a mind that's willing to serve
In appreciation for this gift we could never deserve.
-That's Grace

                            Lillian Colson Graham 2015

Reach Out

Women, Men, children, all
Here's the Universal call
If things seem to be out of control
And the earth is about to fold
Just Reach Out!
If you try to do things right
And everyone wants to fight
Everything turns inside out
Faith turns into doubt
Just Reach Out!
The day is cold, dark, and dreary
I walk but the walk is slow and weary
I walk but the sight is dull and teary
The next step is kinda scary
Just Reach Out!
The job is starting to lay off
The paycheck just does not pay-off
The paycheck does not pay the bills
The income does match the out-go
And the appetite does not match the meals
Just Reach Out!
The teens in the home are no longer mindful
They consider life at home is boring and dull
They don't agree with the things that are safe and clean
Reach Out!
They consider your counsel old, mean, headaches, body aches, feeling ill
Doctor's bill from last visits unpaid still.
Every walk you take seems to be uphill.

LET THERE BE LIGHT

Reach Out!
Fun, laughter exist no more
Everyday life seems to be a bore
Remember, GOD is here, there, everywhere
HE sees every smile and every tear just reach out!

                Lillian Colson Graham 2016

The Gospel

The Birth:
Twas the Night before Christmas
When Christ was born
Yes, He was here on the
First Christmas morn.
   -That's Gospel
His Life:
He grew strong and wise, healing the sick,
raising the dead, Teaching, Directing,
Preaching
   -That's Gospel
His Death:
He went to the Cross, our souls to save
How precious was That Life, He willingly gave.
The Blood, The Blood that washed away our sins.
Our bondage in sin had come to an end.
   -That's Gospel
His Resurrection:
Early on the third day morn
He was raised up again
And Life in this world will never be the same.
   -That's Gospel
His Ascension:
He Lives, He Lives and now He
Returns home above
He now returns to a place filled with Love.
He gave His Life that we might live
We ask ourselves, what can we give.
   -That's Gospel

LET THERE BE LIGHT

His Promise:
He's preparing a place for the worshipping believers
He will come again, He promised
To receive us.
Love, Love how wonderful is Love
It comes to us from the Father above.
   -That's Gospel

                    Lillian Colson Graham 2015

The Church

The body of Christ have you not heard
Have you not read The Spiritual Word.
He will return to receive His Bride
His return will be known on the earth worldwide.
Meanwhile, we must Love Her, support Her in every way
Adore Her, Uplift Her, and for Her we pray.
Keep Her in our thoughts each and every day.
Glue Her with Love, cement Her with godliness
Fill Her with Ministry and
Pant her with holiness.
She is Christ's Bride and for Her He died.
For Her, was a Thorn Crown on His head
And a hole in His side
For Her, His work here was finished
His mission was done.
The battle was over, the victory was won. - For Her
The Church is in the Heart, but
God visited His people in the Temple.-
   -The Church

                Lillian Colson Graham 2015

Repentance

ACKNOWLEDGE all sins before the Father in prayer
*Without prayer what peace we often
Forfeit what needless grief we bare."
Ask The Father To Forgive your Transgressions and sin
Be SORRY and REGRETFUL for an ungodly actions.
Thoughts and deeds what a wonderful God who provides our needs.
Turn Away From worldliness place
Your thoughts on High and Above
Place your sights on the Father's Love
-That's Repentance
When God forgives He cleans the slate.
There is no record of the time or date.
-That's Repentance

                Lillian Colson Graham 2015

Brother – McKinley Jr. (Sonny)

Sister – Maxi B. Sinkler

Chronicled in the local newspaper – Lillian was the program coordinator for the Women's Advisory Committee. This committee was instrumental in seeing women further their careers in the Postal service.

The Greatest of These is Love

Arriving from college to Hartford, Connecticut in 1958, at the same time leaving college in 1958 and returning to Hartford after three years of college in Atlanta, GA, was a "glad-sad" occasion.

At birth, I was given to my mother's cousin and her husband Minnie Lee and Norman Lee cousin. This was a blessing to them since they never had another child. I lived with my great-grandmother who lived in Adel Georgia, and who was the town midwife and who delivered most babies in town (black and white). My father lived in Adel, and was a very popular fellow. He had other children that I knew, McKinley, Jr.(Sonny), James Wesley (Papa), Maxie Bea, and Ann. All of which I knew from a distance. I was his oldest child. My mother had another daughter (Arlene). When my stepfather returned from World War II U.S. Army, I was returned to them (mother dear and daddy) in Tifton, Georgia. After grade school and high school, the family moved to Hartford, Connecticut and soon got divorced.

Glad because I was united with my family and reacquainted with my birth mother and younger sister. Sad because I had worked very hard in school, but my parents could not afford for me to stay. At that time, they knew nothing about student loans. February 2, 1960, I married Charles Henry Graham – I became Lillian Leola Graham. At the same time, I joined Phillips Metropolitan CME Church. The church was small, about 75 to 100 members. I worked on the Trustee Board; organized and sang in the Gospel Chorus; organized the church's first Board of Christian Education; became a Sunday School teacher of the intermediate class; later became teacher of the adult class. I took the youth and young adults to their first National Youth and Young Adult Conference. There we were known as the first place winners of most contests.

To name some—Best Original Rap; Best Original-poem; Best Original drama (puppet show); Scripture Memorization, and Hymn Memorization, just a few of the trophies we brought back to the Hartford Church. These conferences were held every four years, involved Youth and Young Adults from all over the USA, Africa, and Haiti. The age group was twelve to thirty-five. My church would send anywhere from fifteen to twenty delegates. Our first claim to fame for our original rap— "Rappin' for Jesus" (see exhibit #4). To name some of the cities we visited: Louisiana, Missouri, Greenville North Carolina (twice), Birmingham Alabama, Orlando Florida (twice) and Louisville Kentucky. To church, I introduced such programs as: The Calendar Dinner, the African Tea, the Down Home Banquet, the Teen Queen Banquet, the "Cheer-up" Cheerleaders, the Sunshine Gang, organized the first Christian Youth Fellowship and hosted the first Senior Member Fellowship.

I was a Church Trustee through three locations: Mather St to Blue Hills Avenue, to 2550 Main Street to 2500 Main Street. Planned and founded by Rev. James Bernard Walker (Now Bishop of the CME Seventh Episcopal District)

How great is our God?
How bright are his lights?

Work in Hartford

My first job was Connecticut General Life Insurance Co. (now Cigna) as a file clerk, later promoted to group leader, employed by the United States Post Office in 1965 as a distribution clerk, became the first Women's Program Coordinator (as needed) then to Equal Employment Opportunity Specialist for Connecticut (USPS) and Southern Massachusetts in 1984, was appointed selected Post Master of Bloomfield, Connecticut the first Black Woman Post Master in Connecticut level 20 and above Retired 9-1-93. Hallelujah, Blessed Be the name of Jesus. Jesus is the Light of the World. In my retired state, I am still the Adult Sunday School Teacher and Author of a Teen Newsletter "Teen Connection."

In the year 1982, we were a small congregation, worshipping on Blue Hills Ave— Hartford in a small church, we had moved from an even smaller church on Mather Street-Hartford. We were assigned a very young pastor by the name of Reverend James Bernard Walker. From that day forward, we were not allowed to consider ourselves as a small congregation. Reverend Walker brought with him his beautiful wife Delois and daughter, Tiffany. A second daughter, Paris was born in Hartford. The first sermon that I remember Reverend Walker preaching was entitled Whack-a-Mole. The children were taken to an amusement park and there was a game there by that name. The wooden moles were arranged in a circle and a player would hit them with a mallet. You would hit one and another's head would pop up. Sooner or later, if you kept playing and kept playing the prize mole would pop up. Pastor explained that life was just that way. Troubles would "pop up," but sooner or later, the prize will come. This was our second lesson from this young man of God, the first being the change from the small church mentality. A third lesson was that the denomination was a whole lot more than what we knew.

For example, we had never attended a National Youth and Young Adult Conference. In fact, we had never heard of one. In *1984,* we attended our first youth and young adult conference in St. Louis Missouri. The conferences were held every four years and we never missed one since that year. In addition to attending, we were prize winners in every category of competition we entered. Another step out of darkness was the separation of fiction from the real and true spiritual walk. Santa Claus had to be downgraded and eliminated, the easter bunny had to be taken out of the resurrection celebration; and Halloween is meant to be sacred, not scary. Christmas became a celebration of our Savior's birth, not to be shared with any other being either real or fictitious. Easter became a time of sorrow (Good Friday) and then great joy (The Resurrection) to be celebrated by believers in appreciation for eternal life. Now, our pastor (Rev. Walker) is no longer known by us as a young man from Boli Oklahoma. He was now known and recognized as a man of GOD. Sent to us by GOD to lead us "out of darkness into the marvelous light." We were introduced to tithing and sacrifice to replace many fundraising efforts. We were led to read, study, research, and understand the word of GOD. *"Study to show yourself approved."*

Bringing to mind, the saying that:
We listen to half the things we hear.
We understand half the things we listen to
We believe half the things we understand and might I add,
We adapt to half the things we believe.

Now, our directions have been changed, our spiritual motives have been repaired: and our motives are guided by the Holy Spirit. We were ready to move and become a light to the community. In **1998,** we were blessed with a beautiful place of worship at 2550 Main Street-Hartford. A place that represents our love for God, God's love for us. And our pastor's love for us. Another bitter/sweet experience was when Reverend Walker was elevated to the Episcopacy and assigned to be Bishop (Presiding Prelate of the Ninth Episcopal District on the Western side of the United States.) This territory includes Hawaii and Alaska.

We lost and they gained one thing we know is that the
"Light now shines in the West."
"Blest be the tie that binds
our hearts in Christian love
the fellowship of kindred minds
is like to that above."

> *"In all these things we are more than conquerors through Him who loves us."*
> (Romans 8:37)

No one can claim to be spiritual if they have not loved. This is the simplest statement made to describe True Christianity. We may err in many ways do the wrong things, set the wrong goals, be attracted to the wrong people, we err less if our motives and methods are bounded by love. If we do what love requires, we will do no wrong. Love requires compassion, commitment, service, concern, and obedience to God's word. Love is the key that unlocks the hardened heart. We cannot evangelize the unrighteous if we have not love. We cannot grow spiritually if we have not love. We cannot express love if we have not love. The Christian's love must not be confined to one group—it must be universal; it must not be not in response to any human action or gift; it is not limited to those who agree with us in opinions; it must not be limited to those connected by blood relationship; it must not be limited we love intimately. Nor can it be limited to who love us. God is love, therefore the love of a True Christian must resemble his love.

Loving God returns us from our drift toward unrighteousness. It delivers us into the hands of God for his protection, his deliverance, his service, his blessings, his mercies, and his guidance. The love for God leads to obedience; obedience leads to Holiness; Holiness generates growth.

To love GOD is to serve GOD.
To love GOD is to study and obey His word.
To love GOD is to live a righteous life.
To love GOD is to love one another.
To love GOD is to obey GOD.
To love GOD is to love, respect, appreciate, honor, adore, worship, JESUS Christ our Savior.

The Greatest of These Is Love: A Tribute

This "Impact" is dedicated to the memory of a great leader, teacher, preacher, and friend: the Late Senior Bishop Thomas Lanier Hoyt, Jr. Those who knew him—really knew him—loved and respected him for his humility, his humor, his knowledge, his compassion, and his love for people. He and his family: his wife Ocie, his daughter Doria, and his son Tom II, joined us while we worshiped at 700 Blue Hills Avenue Hartford, Conn., our pastor being the Reverend James B. Walker, Now Bishop James B. Walker who at this time, Presiding Prelate of the Ninth Episcopal District of the CME Church). In 1994, when Reverend Doctor Hoyt announced that he was going to be a candidate for bishop, we the members decided that we wanted to help him in his efforts. Although we had no idea what to do or how to do it. After all, we had never been involved in the making of a bishop. However, because of the love we had for him, we did what we did and he made bishop. Later, years, he became Senior Bishop. Whenever he came anywhere near us to teach, to preach or to lecture, we were there also. We could look at this great leader and claim that we helped. We could reminisce about the days when he stood with us, the pastor and congregation, encouraged and supported. I remember his support when the young people attended the National Youth and Young Adult Conferences, when daughter Doria was a part of the PMC Rappers who went "Rappin' for Jesus." His support and his love for those young people gave them the confidence to perform before thousands and win. (See exhibit # 1) Personally, I was the Director of Christian Education at the local church. I put my resignation papers on the pastor's desk. (This happened quite often). This particular time Bishop Hoyt was in town and delivered the Sunday morning sermon his topic was "There Are Rewards and Benefits For Working in the Kingdom: but He has no Retirement Plan." After the service, I, unnoticeably went to the bishop and said to him, "Bishop, people would think you were preaching to or about me." He answered, "Oh no! Mrs. Graham, I was preaching to the whole congregation, but especially to you." That only meant that I had to wait another year, and when he was back in his own Episcopal District, to resign again. It was a bittersweet experience for us when the family moved away to the newly assigned territory. Bitter because we missed a dear friend, and sweet because he made it. I want to share my last correspondence from the bishop with you. This letter was written to me seven months before the bishop moved from labor to reward. (See attachment #2) "Love is the wheel that makes the world go around." We as a race were harmed but not hemmed, we as a race did not have plenty, but we as a race had Jesus. Love is the key that open any heart.

> *"Charity suffereth long and is kind."* (1 Corinthians 13:4)
> *"A friend loveth at all times."* (Proverbs 17:1)

The Moral of the Stories...

The early years – These early years will serve as a warning for parents and guardians. Be careful what you say, what you do, and how you act around young children. Some of them begin to remember things earlier than you realize.

Family and Church Experiences – These are said to be two of God's anointed institutions. If you defame one of them, there are serious consequences. But, if you contribute to the strength and power of each, there are great rewards.

School Daze – The period of good days and bad days. Abilities and talents are discovered, punishment and rewards, laughter and tears, fun poking, mischief, trial and error, joking and teasing, disobedience, etc. However, at this point there are many lessons to be learned. If lessons are not learned there are consequences now and in the future.

Higher education years and/or Work Experiences – The period where the abilities and talents were discovered in an earlier stage and can be developed further and used.

Travels, People Places and Venues – Church Experiences – The stage of life where all rewards are cashed in!! To God be the glory. Look back and see where God was there from the very beginning and there was light!

Exhibit #1
Congratulations to Mrs. Lillian Graham!
April 20, 2013

Words cannot express the great admiration the Hoyt family has for you, Mrs. Lillian Graham. Just the mention of your name signifies excellence, dedication, a lover of children, a first-rate organizer, a servant leader, a Bishop maker, a friend for life, and a Christian woman, who sings and lives positively the underlying question, "If God is dead, what makes my life worth living?" You have told and shown us through your life the one who occupies the center of your life: "Jesus, the Christ."

While Ocie, Doria, Ayanna, Thomas III, and I, as your Bishop, could not be present at this celebration of your life, you must know that we love you dearly. Thanks for showing us how to do Church work and at the same time showing us how to do the Work of the Church. Phillips Metropolitan C.M.E. Church and many of your spiritual children have learned much through your wise counsel and exemplary living. May God continue to give you God's Shalom.

In Christ,
The Hoyt Family

Exhibit # 2
Just A Word!

God is up to something marvelous, majestic, and extraordinary again! Knowledge is the ingredient that sustains us when we are searching for answers in life. Christian Education is the vehicle by which we knowingly move from glory to glory. God has gifted this servant, Mrs. Lillian Graham, to be a depositor of such knowledge. She has certainly been, and continues to be, a resource of ideas, themes, and teaching techniques for generations.

I am proud to have been labeled as one of the four Musketeers in the New York – New England District of our beloved Christian Methodist Episcopal Church. Lillian Graham, Edith Wheeler (deceased), Virginia Edgerton (relocated to Arizona) and I earned the title by demonstrating our ability to be a mighty team of Christian educators back in the day. Lillian would set the pace, and the task became creative, ground breaking biblical challenges and fun. Today, we serve as arm-bearers and a reservoir of resources for others.

Mrs. Graham in this endeavor takes planting, watering, and cultivating a step forward by sharing some of what she has gleaned over the years in print. Thank God for this life-long learner, who has proved herself to be a vessel, a friend, a gift to me, to the C.M.E Church and who ever seeks knowledge in Jesus' name. To God be the glory!

Yvonne L. Patterson
Calvary C.M.E. Church
Buffalo, NY

Exhibit # 3
Valedictorian Speech and Some Wise Sayings from the Valedictorian Speech for Seniors to Be Guided By
May 14, 1954

Tourists in mountainous regions are often fascinated by the feats of daring acts performed by the natives. Up, up, up, over the rocks that seem impossible to the beholder, they climb with agility and ease to the highest point accessible. Clinging to the smallest edge of the rock and finding a foothold upon ledges that are scarcely perceptible. It does not seem remarkable to them. They are schooled to such efforts from their earliest years, and it has become a second nature to them. Sometimes their hands may be torn in grasping some sharp bits of rock, or their feet may be cut by contact with its keen edges on the goal ahead, and they pay but little attention to the rocks that they pass. They do not even question whether or not they can surmount the difficulties in their way. They must surmount them and nothing remains to be said. In our daily lives we too are climbing toward some longed for goals, the obstacles in our path often look as fierce and impossible as the rocks in these mountain gorges, but if we have properly schooled ourselves for the climb, we know that all things are possible of attainment if we are determined upon success. When Napoleon turned from his other European conquests to advance upon Italy, his soldiers rebelled and scoffed at a venture so obviously impossible. "You cannot cross the Alps. It is impossible", they told him. But, did he give into murmuring? No with that determination that characterized this greatest of generals throughout all his career, he answered them grimly, "There shall be no Alps" and led them on to certain victory. This is the spirit that we as independent individuals should meet with all the difficulties that comfort us. Ignore the obstacles and they are already half overcome. Longfellow says, "We have not wings, we cannot soar, but we have feet to scale and climb by slow degree cloudy summits of our time" and the climbing is glorious work. There is such inspiration in every step forward, such a thrill of self-satisfaction in each rock left behind us that we share in part the momentous exaltation as he mounts higher and higher toward the glittering peaks above him which lie. How a prize ahead of us worth stringing for. And keep our eyes presentably fixed upon it, no obstacles in our path can go up. Instead, every hardship encountered spurs us to greater effort, and fires us with a firm determination to conquer any and everything that lies before us.

"*Habit is ten times nature.*"
"*Sadness is the poison of the soul.*"
"*Belief in a future life is the appetite of reason.*"
"*The future is fairyland to the young and holy land to the old.*"
"*We forgive too little, forget to much.*"
"*The wisest man can always learn something from the dumbest person.*"
"*The secret of lies in the respect of the pupil.*"
"*Doubt is hell in the human soul.*"
"*Eat to please thyself; but dress to please others.*"
"*He who purposely cheat his friends would cheat his GOD.*"
"*A good dinner sharpens the wit; and soften the heart.*"
"*A lie that is half a truth is ever the blackest of all lies.*"
"*Lying is a mark of cowardice.*"
"*The worst thing an old man can be is a lover.*"
"*Love's like the measles, worse when it comes late in life.*"
"*We are shaped and fashioned by what we love.*"
"*Love gives itself: it is not bought.*"
"*Little things are great to young men.*"
"*Light is the symbol of truth.*"
"*Human life is a constant want: and should be a constant prayer.*"
"*A kiss from mother is always the sweetest.*"
"*Paradise is open to all kind hearts.*"
"*A jealous man always find more than he looks for.*"
"*He who puts up with insults, invite injury.*"
"*There is time when ignorance is bliss.*"
"*Ideas control the world.*"

"Mine honor is my life."
"We make our habits, then our habits make us."
"Choose your husband life as you do your wedding-gown, for qualities that would wear well."
"He is richest who is content with the least, for content is the wealth of nature."
"I now know that wars do not end wars."
"Better three hours too soon, than one minute too late."
"To choose time is to save time."
"Second thoughts, they say are best."
"Good taste is the flower of good sense."
"The unspoken word does not harm."
"Fellows who have no tongue are usually all ears and eyes."
"Doubt whom you may, but never doubt yourself."
"GOD heals and the doctor takes the fee."
"Our opportunity to do good are our talents."
"Music is the medicine of a broken heart."
"He that is down need not fear a fall."
"It is much better to learn men than to learn man."
"Men, in general are but children."
"Sin has many tools, but a lie is a handle that fits them all."
"Jazz will endure as long as people hear it through their feet instead of their brains."
"I had six honest serving men - they taught me all I knew: Their names were where and what and when - and why and how and who."
"Life will teach you to think but thinking will not teach you to live."
"It ain't no use putting up your umbrella until it rains. That is the definition of worry."
"If you want to kill any idea in the world, get a committee to work on it."
"Some people are so afraid to die that they never begin to live."
"Debate is the death of a conversation."
"People generally quarrel because they cannot argue."
"Trust not the world for it never payeth what it promiseth."
"The only fence against the world is a thorough knowledge of it."
"Idle blows the wind that profits nobody."
"It is the will that makes the doing good or bad."

"Whiskey is a good thing in its place, there is nothing like it for preserving a man when he is dead, if you want to keep a dead man put him in whiskey, if you want to kill a live man put whiskey in him."
"Those who exaggerate their statements belittle themselves."
"Where the speech is corrupted the mind is also.
"Yesterday has gone. Forget it. Tomorrow hasn't come. Think of it. Today is here. Use it."
"Love is like a rose, beautiful today and tomorrow gone to some unknown world."
"Acquaint yourself with the personality twins. Meet behavior and be good."
"Stolen kisses are always sweeter."
"I envy no man that knows more than myself, but pity them that know less."
"What is not fully understood is not passed."
"Manners are stronger than laws."
"A man finds himself seven years older the day after marriage."
"Pride is the master sin of the devil."
"Wishing is the constant hectic of the fool."
"Every wish is like a prayer with GOD."
"Hating people is like burning down your own house to get rid of the rats."
"A man isn't poor if he can still laugh."

Exhibit #4
Rapping for Jesus

We came to bring good news to you.
To tell the bling that they can see.
To tell the poor how rich they could be.
Born one day in Bethlehem in a little manger,
There was no room for him inside and others called him a stranger.
He called twelve disciples to walk with him
Through the streets of Jerusalem.
He called Andrew and Peter his brother.
He didn't stop there, he called ten others.
He called James and John,
Zebedee's two sons,
Then the tax collector Matthew.

LET THERE BE LIGHT

Philip, Thomas, Bartholomew,
But still there was more work to do.
James, Thaddeus and a zealot called Simon.
And then there was Judas
Now the real work has begun
Jesus went about preaching, teaching, and reaching the lost
Healing, saving, and the blessing with no cost.
Jesus taught about the speck and the log.
You have no right to judge others at all.
Jesus taught about man's meditation,
Where money was his one and only dedication.
Then he talked about the Samaritan man
Who always lent a helping hand.
Then he came to the narrow gate.
The way was easy but very straight.
At the end of his life his mother cried.
He hung his head and died.
That's our salvation.

Sister Lillian wrote and orchestrated a group of young
ladies in the church, "Rapping for Jesus"

The Value of Bible Knowledge

"The earth shall be full of the knowledge of the LORD as the waters cover the Sea."

(Isaiah 11:9)

The Holy Bible is a friend that inspires from beginning to end. The Holy Bible is a guide.

Its words in which we shall confide.

Lights

Fun time in Christ is a learning tool
Can be used in youth groups and Sunday School
Can be used with Adults, to lose them
Just as long as someone learns something about "Him."

Son Lights (KJV)

JESUS, JESUS, JESUS
O what a wonderful Son
JESUS, JESUS, JESUS
Through you the victory is won
JESUS, JESUS, JESUS
We love You, Yes I do
We came into salvation all because of you!
—Lillian Colson Graham (2015)

I am The Good Shepherd
John 10:11–14

I am The Bread of Life
John 6:35,48

I am The Way The Truth and The Life
John 14:6

I am The Door of The Sheep
John 10:7

I am The Resurrection and The Life
John 11:25

I am The True Vine,
John 15:1

I Am The Light of The World
John 8:12

I Am He-
John 8:28 and
John 13:19

I Am He
John 4:26

I Am The Living Bread which came down from Heaven.
John 6:51

Simon Peter said: *We believe and are sure that Thou art that Christ, The Son of The Living GOD.*
John 6:69

I Am in the Father, and the Father in Me ...
John 14:11

Man doth not live by bread only.
Deut. 8:3

JESUS:
Let not your heart be troubled; ye believe in GOD, believe also in me.
John 14:1

JESUS:
And I, if I be lifted up from the earth, will draw all men unto ME.
John 12:32

JESUS:
For the poor always ye have with you, but Me ye have not always.
John 12:8

JESUS:
If ye love Me keep my commandments.
John 14:15

JESUS:
I will not leave you comfortless: I will come to you.
John 14:18

Search Lights (KJV)

If there are things we need to know!
And we don't know where to go
You may turn on the Search Light
Turn that Light on day or night
Find what you are looking for
About the Father, The Spirit, or The Savior

JESUS' warnings and woes to the Pharisees.
Matthew 13:23–39

Miracles on the day JESUS died.
Matthew 27:31–53

The Execution of John the Baptist
Mark 6:21

JESUS: Future events foretold
Mark 2:8

The Transfiguration
Matthew 28:19-20
Mark 9:2-5

JESUS: The signs of the end of This Age.
Mark 12:13

The Angels and the Shepherds
Luke 2:8

The Crucifixion of Jesus
Luke 23:44
Matthew 27:32
Mark 15:21

The Resurrection of Jesus
Mark 16:1
Matthew 28:1

The seven last words of Jesus on the cross.
Luke 23:33–43,46
John 19:27

List of Disciples
Act 1:13

Ten Commandments
Exodus 20:1–17

The Creation
Genesis 1:1
Psalms 51:10
Col. 1:16

Jesus blesses the little children
Matthew 19:13

The Triumphal entry into Jerusalem
Matthew 21:45

The Cleansing of the Temple by Jesus
Matthew 21:12–13

Barren Fig Tree
Matthew 21:18–20

The faithful and unfaithful servants.
Matthew 25:45–51

The Ascension of Jesus
Luke 24:51
Acts 1:6-11
Mark 16:19
1 Cor. 15:6

The Beatitudes
Matthew 5:3–12

Anointing of Jesus at Bethany—The Alabaster box.
Matthew 26:6
Mark 14:1

Bargain of Judas Iscariot.
Matthew 26:14–16

Agony in Gethsemane
Matthew 26:73
Mark 14:32

Peter's Denial
Matthew 26:69–74

The Transfiguration
Mark 9:2-5
Matthew 28:19–20

The Cleansing of the Temple
Mark 11:12

The Widow's mite
Mark 12:41

Birth of John the Baptist foretold
Luke 1:19

The Birth of Jesus foretold
Luke 1:26

Christian Life
Luke 23:32–46

The Ten Plagues of Egypt
Exodus 7:14, 11:1

Potter's Field
Matthew 27:3–10
Acts 1:18,19

Joshua and the children of Israel cross the Jordan river
Joshua 3:1

The Fruit of the Spirit
Galatians 5:22,23

The Lord's Prayer—the Model Prayer
Matthew 6:9–13
Luke 11:2–4

The Last Supper—Communion
Matthew 26:17-35

The Exodus from Egypt-40 years
Chapters 20, 32–33, 35–40 Books of Exodus

The sins of Lot's daughters
Genesis 30–38

Adam and Eve
Genesis 2:4–9

Bright Lights (KJV)

JESUS:

> "The people that walked in the darkness have seen a great light: they that dwell in the land of the shadow of death, upon them hath the light shined."
> (Isaiah 9:2)

Peter:

> "Thou art the Christ, the Son of the Living GOD."
> (Matthew 16:16)

The Transfiguration
Matthew 17:1–4

The Almighty GOD speaks through Isaiah—major prophet:

> "For my thoughts are not your thoughts, neither are your ways my ways saith the LORD. For as the Heavens are higher than the earth, so are My ways higher than your ways and My thoughts than your thoughts."
> (Isaiah 55:8-9)

LET THERE BE LIGHT

Paul to the Church at Rome:

> "For The Kingdom of GOD is not meat and drink; but righteousness, and peace, and joy in the Holy Ghost."
> (Romans 14:17)

Paul to the Roman Church:

> "For I reckon that the sufferings of this present time are not worthy to be compared with the glory which shall be revealed in us."
> (Romans 8:18) KJV

Paul to the Church at Philippi:

> "For me to live is CHRIST, and to die is gain."
> (Philippians 1:21)

Paul to the Church at Ephesus:

> "Be ye angry, and sin not."
> (Ephesians 4:26)

Paul's Letter to Timothy:

> "GOD hath not given us the spirit of fear, but of power, and of love…"
> (2 Timothy 1:7)

Isaiah:

> "The son shall be no more thy light by day, neither for brightness shall the moon give light unto thee; but the LORD shall be unto thee an everlasting light, and thy GOD the glory."
> (Isaiah 60:19)

Jesus:

> "*Greater love hath no man than this, that a man lay down his life for his friend.*"
> (John 15:13)

Jesus:

> "*And ye shall know the truth and the truth shall make you free.*"
> (John 8:32)

Jesus:

> "*But I say unto you, love your enemies.*"
> (Matthew 5:44)

Jesus:

> "*But I know Him: for I am from Him, and He hath sent Me.*"
> (John 7:29)

Jesus:

> "*But I said unto you, that ye also have seen me and believe not ME.*"
> (John 6:36)

Jesus:

> "*Let not your heart be troubled, you believe in GOD, believe also in Me in My Father's house are many mansions. If it were not so, I would have told you. I go to prepare a place. And if I go to prepare*

a place for you, I will come again and receive you to myself. That where I am, there you may be also."
(John 14:1–4)

Ceiling Lights (KJV)

With these lights, look up toward the Father
In these lights, we one day hope to gather in these lights, with
hope and expectation.
In these lights is reward for dedication
In these lights we bow in adoration
In these lights is cause for celebration

Jesus:

"Not everyone that saith unto me, LORD, LORD shall enter the Kingdom of Heaven. But he that doeth the will of My Father which is in Heaven."
(Matthew 7:21)

Jesus said:

"Verily, verily, I say unto thee except a man be born again he cannot see the Kingdom of GOD."
(John 3:3)

To Nicodemus.

"Except a man be born of water and of the Spirit, he cannot enter into the Kingdom of GOD."
(John 3:5)

Jesus said:

"GOD is a Spirit and they that worship HIM must worship HIM in Spirit and in truth."
(John 4:24)

Jesus:

> "In my Father's house are many mansions: if it were not so I would have told you. I go to prepare a place for you. And if I go to prepare a place for you, I will come again and receive you unto myself, that where I am, there you may be also."
> (John 14:2–3)

Voice from Heaven:

> "This is my Beloved Son in whom I am well pleased."
> (Matthew 3:17)

Job in His Speech During His Suffering:

> "There the wicked cease from troubling; and there weary be at rest."
> (Job 3:17)

Job's Response to His Friend Zophar:

> "Though He slay me, yet will I trust in HIM: but I will maintain mine own ways before Him."
> (Job 13:15)

Job in His Reply to His Friend Bildad:

> "For I know that my Redeemer liveth, and that HE shall stand at the latter day upon the earth."
> (Job 19:25)

Isaiah (Major Prophet):

> "Seek ye the LORD while HE may be found, call ye upon HIM while HE is near."
> (Isaiah 55:6)

LET THERE BE LIGHT

Isaiah (Major Prophet):

> *"Every valley shall be exalted, and every mountain and hill shall be made low: and crooked shall be made straight, and the rough places plain:"*
> (Isaiah 40:4)

Dim Lights

God will give us the strength to resist.
He gave his Commandments in the form of a list
Woe to the Scribes and to the Pharisees that we don't pattern our lives after them.
Let us be sure that our lights are not dim, that our lives are patterned only after him.

> *"Be not deceived: evil communications corrupt good manners."*
> (1 Corinthians 15:33)

Jesus:

> *"For JESUS testified, that a prophet hath no honour in his own country"*
> (John 4:44)

Jesus:

> *"Have not I chosen you twelve, and one of you is a devil."*
> (John 6:70)

> *"JESUS wept."*
> (John 11:35)

Jesus:

"The Harvest truly is plenteous, but the laborers are few;"
(Matthew 9:37)

Jesus:

"So shall it be at the end of the world: the Angels shall come forth, and sever the wicked from among The Just, and shall cast them into the furnace of fire: there shall be wailing and gnashing of teeth."
(Matthew 13:49–50)

Jesus:

"And this gospel of the Kingdom shall be preached in all the world for a witness unto all nations; and then shall the end come."
(Matthew 24:14)

Jesus:

"Woe unto, you Scribes and Pharisees hypocrites! for ye compass sea and land to make one proselyte, and when he is made, ye make him twofold more the child of hell than yourselves."
(Matthew 23:15)

Jesus:

"But woe be unto you Scribes and Pharisees, hypocrites! For ye shut up the Kingdom of Heaven against men: for ye neither go in yourselves neither suffer ye them that are entering to go in."
(Matthew 23:13)

Jesus:

> *"Woe unto you, ye blind guides, which say, whosoever shall swear by the temple, it is nothing; but whosoever shall swear by the gold of the temple, he is a debtor!"*
>
> (Matthew 23:16)

Jesus:

> *"Woe unto you Scribes and Pharisees, hypocrites! for ye pay tithes of mint and anise and cummin and have omitted the weightier matters of the law, judgment, mercy, and faith: these ought ye to have done, and not to leave the other undone."*
>
> (Matthew 23:23)

Jesus:

> *"Woe unto you Scribes and Pharisees, hypocrites! For ye make clean the outside of the cup and of the platter, but within they are full of extortion and excess."*
>
> (Matthew 23:25–26)

Jesus:

> *"Woe unto you, Scribes, Pharisees, hypocrites! For ye are like unto whited sepulchres, which indeed appear beautiful outward, but are within full of dead men's bones, and of all uncleanness."*
>
> (Matthew 23:27)

Job to His Friend Zophar

> *"Man that is born of a woman is of few days and full of trouble."*
>
> (Job 14:1)

De-Lights

Verses from the book of Psalms, the largest book in the Bible, words of power and praise.
(150 Chapters)

> *"For in the time of trouble HE shall hide me in his Pavilion, in the secret of his tabernacle shall HE hide me. HE shall set me up upon a rock."*
> (Psalms 27:5)

> *"The LORD is my light and my salvation; whom shall I fear? The LORD is the strength of my life; whom shall I be afraid?"*
> (Psalms 27:1)

> *"Be of good courage, and HE shall strengthen your heart, all ye that hope in the LORD."*
> (Psalms 31:24)

> *"I will bless the LORD at all times: HIS praise shall continually be in my mouth."*
> (Psalms 34:1)

> *"The Angel of the LORD encampeth round about them that fear HIM, and delivereth them."*
> (Psalms 34:7)

> *"The steps of a good man are ordered by the LORD and he delighteth in his way."*
> (Psalms 37:23)

> *"I have been young, and now am old; yet have I not seen the righteous forsaken, nor his seed begging bread."*
> (Psalms 37:25)

"A little that a righteous man hath is better than the riches of many wicked."
(Psalms 37:16)

"Blessed is he that considereth the poor: the LORD will deliver him in time of trouble."
(Psalms 41:1)

"Be still, and know that I am GOD: I will exalted among the heathen, I will be exalted in the earth."
(Psalms 46:10)

"For a day in Thy courts is better than a thousand, I had rather be a doorkeeper in the house of my GOD than to dwell in the tents of wickedness."
(Psalms 84:10)

"For a thousand years in Thy sight are but as yesterday when it is past, and as a watch in the night."
(Psalms 90:4)

"The days of our years are threescore years and ten, and if by reason of strength they be fourscore years, yet is their strength labor and sorrow, for it is soon cut off, and we soon fly away."
(Psalms 90:10)

"So teach us to number our days that we may apply our hearts unto wisdom."
(Psalms 90:12)

"What shall I render unto the LORD for all HIS benefits towards me? I will take the cup of Salvation, and call upon the name of the LORD. I will pay my vows unto the LORD now in the presence of all HIS people."
(Psalms 116:12–14)

"This is the day which the LORD hath made. We will rejoice and be glad in it."
(Psalms 118:24)

"Delight thyself also in the LORD, and HE shall give the desires of thine heart."
(Psalms 37:4)

Verses From the Book of Proverbs:
(Written to Make the Wise Wiser)

"The rich and poor meet together the LORD is the maker of them all."
(Proverbs 22:2)

"Train up a child in the way he should go and when he is old he will not depart from it."
(Proverbs 22:6)

"For riches certainly make themselves wings, they fly away as an eagle toward heaven."
(Proverbs 23:5)

"A drunkard and the glutton shall come to poverty and drowsiness shall clothe a man with rags."
(Proverbs 23:21)

"Boast not thyself of tomorrow; for thou knowest not what a day may bring forth."
(Proverbs 27:1)

Flashing Lights (KJV)

A Good word here, a good word there
A good word is needed everywhere
Turn on this light and save some souls

LET THERE BE LIGHT

Turn on this light, reach Holy goals
Turn on this light, and be ye fed
JESUS Christ is our daily bread.

John:
Behold the Lamb of GOD, which taketh away the sins of the world.

Jesus:

> *"How much then is a man better than a sheep? Wherefore it is lawful to do well on the Sabbath days."*
> (Matthew 12:12)

Jesus:

> *"Wherefore I say unto you, all manner of sin and blasphemy shall be forgiven unto men: but the blasphemy against the Holy Ghost shall not be forgiven unto men. And whosoever speaketh a word against the Son of man, it shall be forgiven him: but whosoever speaketh the Holy Ghost, it shall not be forgiven him, neither in this world, neither in the world to come."*
> (Matthew 12:31–32)

Paul to the Church of Rome:

> *"Recompense to no man evil for evil."*
> (Romans 12:17)

Jesus:

> *"Not that which goeth into the mouth defileth a man, but that which cometh out of the mouth, this defileth a man."*
> (Matthew 15:11)

Jesus:

> "For where two or three are gathered together in my name, there am I in the midst of them."
> (Matthew 18:20)

Jesus:

> "Verily I say unto you, whatsoever ye shall bind on earth shall be bound in Heaven. And whatsoever ye shall loose on earth shall be loosed in Heaven."
> (Matthew 18:18)

Jesus:

> "For this cause shall a man leave Father and Mother, and shall cleave to his wife and they twain shall be one flesh?"
> (Matthew 19:5)

Jesus:

> "And again I say unto you, it is easier for a camel to go through the eye of a needle than for a rich man to enter the Kingdom of GOD."
> (Matthew 19:24)

And Jesus answering said unto them:

> "They that are whole need not a physician; but they that are sick."
> (Luke 5:31)

Jesus:

"I came not to call the righteous, but sinners to repentance."
(Luke 5:32)

Jesus:

"Peace I leave with you, my peace I give unto you, not as the world giveth, give I unto you. Let not your heart be troubled, neither let it be afraid."
(John 14:27)

1. When Naaman was cured of the leprosy, to what liar was the leprosy given?

    - 2 Kings 5:25–27
    - Gehazi

God's Judgment Against Judah:

Isaiah 5:8-23 (KJV)

> 8-Woe unto them that join house to house that lay field to field, till there be no place, that they may be placed alone in the midst of the earth!
> 9- In mine ears said the Lord of hosts, Of a truth many houses shall be desolate, even great and fair, without inhabitant.
> 10- Yea, ten acres of vineyard shall yield one bath, and the seed of an homer shall yield an ephah.
> 11-Woe unto those who rise up early in the morning, that they may follow strong drink; that continue until night, till wine inflame them!
> 12- And the harp, and the viol, the tabret, and pipe, and wine, are in their feasts: but they regard not the

work of the LORD, neither consider the operation of his hands.

13- Therefore my people are gone into captivity, because they have no knowledge: and their honourable men are famished, and their multitude dried up with thirst.

14- Therefore hell hath enlarged herself, and opened her mouth without measure: and their glory, and their multitude, and their pomp, and he that rejoiceth, shall descend into it.

15- And the mean man shall be brought down, and the mighty man shall be humbled, and the eyes of the lofty shall be humbled:

16- But the LORD of hosts shall be exalted in judgment, and God that is holy shall be sanctified in righteousness.

17- Then shall the lambs feed after their manner, and the waste places of the fat ones shall strangers eat.

18- Woe unto them that draw iniquity with cords of vanity, and sin as it were with a cart rope.

19- That say, Let him make speed, and hasten his work, that we may see it: and let the counsel of the Holy One of Israel draw nigh and come, that we may know it!

20- Woe unto them that call evil good, and good evil; that put darkness for light, and light for darkness; that put bitter for sweet, and sweet for bitter!

21- Woe unto them that are wise in their own eyes, and prudent in their own sight!

22- Woe unto them that are mighty to drink wine, and men of strength to mingle strong drink:

23- Which justify the wicked for reward, and take away the righteousness of the righteous from him!

2. Who sang the victory song after Egyptians were drowned in the Red Sea?

   – Exodus 15:20
   – Miriam

3. Besides Moses's whose rods turned into serpents?

    – Exodus 7:8–12
    – Aaron and the Egyptian Magicians

4. Whose name means Day Star?

    – Isaiah 14:1–12
    – Lucifer

5. Who killed two people at once with one spear?

    – Numbers 25:7–8
    – Phinehas (Aaron's grandson)

6. What two people had years added to their life span?

    – 2 Kings 20:9–11
    – King Hezekiah and Joshua
    – Joshua 10:12–14

7. What three things did God tell Moses to do at the burning bush?

    – Exodus 3:5 and Exodus 4:4–7
    – Take off his sandals
    – Pick up his rod
    – And put his hand in his bosom

8. What happen to the Philistine who stole the Ark of the Covenant?

    – 1 Samuel 5:11–12
    – They were smitten with tumors and died

9. What man did God strike dead for refusing to help David?

    – 1 Samuel 25:38
    – Nabal

10. What bad man got his head nailed to the ground?

    – Judges 4:17–21
    – Sisera

11. When told that his sons had been killed and the Ark of the Covenant had been taken who fell over backward and died of a broken neck?

    – 1 Samuel 4:16–18
    – Eli

12. What was the name of the idol that kept falling on his face in front of the Ark of the Covenant?

    – 1 Samuel 5:3–5
    – Dagon

13. What two Old Testament figures did not die?

    – Genesis 5:24 (God took) Enoch
    – 2 Kings 2:1, 11 (Whirlwind) Elijah

14. Who was Noah's great-grandfather?

    – Genesis 5:22–29
    – Enoch (Enoch was the Father of Methuselah)

15. What King claimed Ruth and Boaz as his great-grandparents?

    – Ruth 4:17
    – David

16. What two men told foreign Kings that their wives were their sisters?

    - Genesis 12:11–13 and Genesis 26:7–11
    - Abraham and Isaac

17. What Judge of Israel had seventy sons?

    - Judges 8:29–30
    - Gideon

18. Who offered to sacrifice his daughter for God?

    - Judges 11:30–31, 34
    - Jephthah

19. Which of the twelve tribes was the first to set foot in the Promised Land?

    - Joshua 3:6
    - Levi

20. How did Jesus refer to the twelve tribes?

    - Matthew 10:6
    - His lost sheep of the house of Israel

21. Which of the twelve tribes established an idolatrous cult?

    - Dan
    - Judges?:18

22. What was the function of the Levites who were not priest?

    - Numbers 3:5–8
    - They took care of the physical maintenance of the tabernacle or temple

23. What tribe did John the Baptist come from?

    - Luke 1:5–13
    - Levi (Since his father was a priest)

24. What New Testament book is addressed to the twelve tribes?

    - James
    - James 1:1

25. What was the tribe of Benjamin famous for?

    - They had left-handed men, who could throw a stone at a hair and not miss.
    - Judges 20:16

26. What tribe was identified as half tribe?

    - Manasseh tribe (because a river divided the tribe)
    - Deut. 3:13

27. How many children did Job have?

    - 20 total—10 were killed and he had 10 more
    - Job 1:2
    - Job 42:13

28. How many windows and doors did Noah's Ark have?

    - 1 of each
    - Genesis 6:16

29. How many souls were saved on the day of Pentecost?

    - About three thousand
    - Acts 2:41

30. What five books of the Bible have only one chapter?

    - Obadiah
    - Philemon
    - 2 John
    - 3 John
    - Jude

31. How old was Noah when the flood came?

    - 600 years old
    - Genesis 7:11

32. Who were the only two people Paul said he baptized?

    - Crispus (leader of the synagogue at Corinth)
    - Gaius (Corinthian believer)
    - 1 Corinthians 1:14

33. Who was a friend of God?

    - Abraham
    - James 2:23

34. What was cursed by God because of Adam?

    - The Ground
    - Genesis 3:17

35. When Elijah was on Mt. Horeb, what three things did God show him?

    - Mighty wind,
    - Earthquake, and
    - Fire
    - 1 Kings 19:11–12

36. What are the seven things God hates?

    - A proud look,
    - A lying tongue,
    - Hands that shed innocent blood,
    - Heart that devises wicked imaginations,
    - Feet that are swift in running to mischief,
    - A false witness who speaks lies,
    - And he who sows discord among the brethren.
    - Proverbs 6:16–19

37. What did Rachel first name Benjamin?

    - Ben-Oni
    - Genesis 35:18

38. What disciple was also known as Levi?

    - Matthew
    - Mark 2:14

39. Who was the first Prophet?

    - Moses
    - Numbers 12:6–8

40. Who was the Prophet who ate the word of the Lord?

    - Ezekiel
    - Ezekiel 2:8–9
    - Ezekiel 3:3

Guiding Lights (KJV)

The word is filled with wisdom and blessings
The word is complete, there is no guessing

LET THERE BE LIGHT

The word will keep you from going astray
The word will teach you GOD's will and way.

Paul to the Church at Corinth:

> *"Therefore, my beloved brethren, be ye steadfast, unmovable, always abounding in the work of the LORD forasmuch as ye know that your labour is not in vain in the LORD."*
>
> (1 Corinthians 15:58)

Isaiah (Major Prophet)

> *But they that wait upon the LORD shall renew their strength, they shall mount up with wings as eagles, they shall run, and not be weary, and they shall walk and not faint.*
>
> (Isaiah 40:31)

Major Prophet:

> *Let the wicked forsake his ways, and the unrighteous man his thoughts: and let him return unto the LORD and HE will have mercy upon him, and to our GOD, for He will abundantly pardon.*
>
> (Isaiah 55:7)

Paul To the Church at Colossians:

> *Set your affection on things above, not on things on the earth.*
>
> (Colossians 3:2)

Paul To the Church at Colossians:

Let your speech be always with grace seasoned with salt, that ye may know how ye ought to answer every man.
(Colossians 4:6)

Paul's Letter To the Church at Corinth:

Come out from among them, and be ye separate, saith the LORD, and touch not the unclean thing; and I will receive you.
(2 Corinthians 6:17)

Paul to the Church at Ephesus:

Be ye angry, and sin not.
(Ephesians 4:26) NIV

Paul to the Church at Ephesus:

Now unto HIM that is able to do exceeding abundantly above all that we ask or think, according to the power that worketh in us, unto HIM be glory in the church by Christ JESUS throughout all ages world without end. Amen
Ephesians 3:20,21

King Solomon's Proverbs:

"A fool uttereth all his mind: but a wise man keepeth it in till afterwards."
(Proverbs 29:11)

James to the Scattered Twelve Tribes:

> "Submit yourselves therefore to GOD. Resist the devil, and he will flee from you. Draw nigh to GOD, and HE will draw nigh to you."
>
> (James 4:7,8) KJV

Paul:

> "For I have learned, in whatsoever state I am, therewith to be content."
>
> (Philippians 4:11)

Paul to the Church at Corinth:

> "Be ye not unequally yoked together with unbelievers: for what fellowship hath righteousness with unrighteousness? And what communion hath light and darkness?"
>
> (2 Corinthians 6:14)

Head Lights (KJV):

Scriptures Tailored to Your Needs!

Bible knowledge comes in several different forms.
This is just one more way to become familiar with God's words, His character, his promises, and his plan for our lives.

1. The Need to be Forgiven

    – John 1:7
    – John 1:9

2. When Thinking about Abortion

    - Psalms 127:3
    - Psalms 139:13–16

3. Involved in Adultery

    - John 8:11
    - Hebrews 13:4

4. HIV/AIDS—God's Love

    - John 11:25
    - John 14:1–3

5. The Alcoholic

    - 1 Corinthians 10:13
    - 1 Corinthians 15:33

6. Angry—Out of Control

    - Ephesians 4:27
    - Colossians 3:8

7. Harmful Habits

    - James 4:7,8
    - 2 Timothy 2:15

8. Abusing Children

    - Matthew 19:14
    - 1 Peter 5:7

9. Life After Death

    - John 14:1-3
    - 1 Corinthians 2:9,10

10. When Burdened Down

    - 2 Corinthians 4:8,9
    - Galatians 2:20

11. Thinking about Divorce

    - Proverbs 18:22
    - Romans 7:2
    - 1 Peter 1:7

12. Problems with Drugs

    - Romans 6:11–13
    - James 1:14–19
    - 1 Peter 4:3

13. Reasons Not to Fear

    - Isaiah 4:10
    - Romans 8:15,16

14. Money Problems

    - Matthew 6:33
    - Philippians 4:19

15. Going through Bereavement

    - John 14:1–3
    - 2 Corinthians 5:2
    - 2 Samuel 12:23

16. For the Homosexual Sisters and Brothers

    - 1 Corinthians 6:1
    - Hebrews 2:18

17. Incest

    - Matthew 19:14
    - Proverbs 3:5,6

18. Are You Lonesome?

    - Matthew 28:20
    - Psalms 40:1–5

19. Are You Facing Temptations?

    - James 1:12-15
    - Romans 8:26

Stop Lights

Jesus:

> *"Judge not, and ye shall not be judged: condemn not, and ye shall not be condemned: forgive, and ye shall be forgiven:"*
>
> Luke 6:37

Jesus:

> *"Give, and it shall be given unto you; good measure pressed down, and shaken together, and running over, shall men give unto your bosom. For with the same measure that ye mete withal it shall be measured to you again."*
>
> Luke 6:38

From the Book of Psalms

> *"Mercy and truth are met together; Righteousness and peace have kissed each other."*
>
> Psalms 85:10

Malachi (Minor Prophet)
(Last Book in the Old Testament)

> *"Will a man rob GOD? Yet ye have robbed me. But ye say, wherein have we robbed thee? In tithes and offerings."*
>
> Malachi 3:8

Malachi (Minor Prophet)
(Last Book in the Old Testament)

> *"Bring ye all the tithes into the storehouse, that there may be meat in mine house, and prove me now herewith, saith the LORD of Hosts, if I will not open you the open windows of Heaven and pour you out a blessing, that there shall not be room enough to receive it."*
>
> Malachi 3:10

We know that all things work together for them ...

More Bible Knowledge

Mountains Information

Mt. Horeb—Alternate name for Mt. Sinai (mountains of God) (Exodus 3:1)

Mt. Sinai—(also called Mt. Horeb)
Where God published the commandments. (Exodus 20:1 and Exodus 23:19).
Also this where God revealed himself to Moses. (Exodus 3:1–10)

Also where God established his covenant with Israel. (Exodus 24:4–18)

Mt. Calvary—(same as Golgotha means skull)
Place where Jesus was crucified. (Luke 23:33)
Golgotha. (Matthew 27:33)

Mt. of Olives—(same as Olivet) A range of hills east of Jerusalem (Matthew 21:11)
Olivet (Acts 1:12) two-mile long ranges east of Jerusalem.
Place of Ezekiel's vision of divine glory (Ezekiel 11:23)
Place of Jesus's Ascension (Acts 1:12)

Mt. Zion—Where David built his palace (2 Samuel 5:69) near where Solomon built the temple
(1 Kings 8:1) names sometimes extended to whole city of Jerusalem.

Mt. Moriah—Place Isaac's sacrifice (Genesis 22:2)
Identified with the site of the temple (2 Chron. 3:1)

Miracles (KJV)

- Water made into wine in Cana

    John 2:1–11
    Matthew 14:15

- Feeding the five thousand

    John 6:1–14
    Mark 6:35
    Luke 9:12
    Matthew 14:15

- Jesus walked on the sea (Going toward Capernaum)

    Matthew 14:22
    Mark 6:47
    John 6:16

- Jesus raises Lazarus from the dead.

    John 11:38–44

- Jesus healed the blind man

    John 9:6,7

- Jesus stilled the storm

    Matthew 8:26,27
    Mark 4:35
    Luke 8:22

- Jesus cast out devils

    Matthew 8:28-32
    Mark 1:16-26

- JESUS healed a man with Palsy

    Matthew 9:2
    Mark 2:1
    Luke 5:18

- JESUS raised the ruler's daughter

    Matthew 9:19-23
    Mark 5:22
    Luke 8:44

- JESUS healed the woman with the issue of blood.

    Matthew 9:20-22
    Mark 2:1
    Luke 5:18

- But when JESUS knew: (That the Pharisees held Council against Him) He withdrew Himself from thence and great multitudes followed Him, and He healed them all.

    Matthew 12:14,15
    Mark 1:32

- JESUS healed the man with a withered hand on the Sabbath.

    Matthew 12:10
    Mark 3:1
    Luke 6:6

- JESUS feeds four thousand-seven loads of bread and a few little fishes-

    Matthew 15:36,37

- JESUS healed the lame, the blind, the dumb, the maimed and many others.

    Matthew 15:30
    Mark 1:32

- JESUS healed Peter's Mother-in-law

    Matthew 8:14
    Mark 1:29
    Luke 4:38

- JESUS healed wild man of Gadara

    Matthew 8:28
    Mark 5:1
    Luke 8:26

- JESUS healed blind Bartimaeus

    Mark 10:46
    Luke 18:35

- Jesus healed the bent over woman

    Luke 13:11

- Jesus healed Malchus ear

    Luke 22:50

- Jesus healed the royal official's son

    John 4:46

- Jesus healed the ten lepers

    Luke 17:11

- Jesus healed the man with dropsy

    Luke 14:1

- Jesus caused the large catch of fish

    Luke 5:4
    John 21:1

- Jesus raised a widow's son

    Luke 7:11

- Jesus healed the lame man at Bethesda

    John 5:1

- Jesus healed a deaf, speechless man

    Mark 7:31

- Jesus heals the Syro Phoenicians daughter

    Matthew 15:21
    Mark 7:24

- Jesus fed 5,000 men and women and children

    Matthew 14:15
    Mark 6:35
    Luke 9:12
    John 6:1

- Jesus heals Jairus's daughter

    Matthew 9:23
    Mark 5:22
    Luke 8:43

- Jesus heals the Centurion's servant

    Matthew 8:5
    Luke 7:1

- Jesus raised the widow's son

    Luke 7:11

Parables

- The Sower—Spreading the word

    Matthew 13:3–9
    Mark 4:3-10

- About the Kingdom of Heaven

    Matthew 13:33–35
    Mark 4:21–31

- Parables of the tares—good seeds and bad seeds

  Matthew 36–40

- Parables about the Kingdom continued

  Matthew 13:44–50

- The parable of the lost sheep

  Matthew 18:10–12

- The parable of the unforgiving servant

  Matthew 18:23

- The worker in the vineyard

  Matthew 20:1–15

- The parable of the two sons

  Matthew 21:28

- The parable of the husbandmen

  Matthew 21:33–41

- The parable of the marriage dinner

  Matthew 22:1–13

- The parable of the Prodigal son
- The parables of the ten virgins

    Matthew 25:1–13

- The parable of the talents

    Matthew 25:14–30

The Twelve Tribes of Israel

The descendants of the twelve sons of Jacob (Renamed Israel by GOD). The Promised Land was divided between the tribes.
They were:

Son's of Jacob and Leah:

1. Reuben—oldest son, talked the brothers out of killing Joseph.
2. Simeon
3. Levi (The Priests—first to enter the Promised Land)
4. Judah (One of the tribes to remain in the Southern Kingdom after the division. The Southern Kingdom was named Judah.)
5. Isachar
6. Zebulon
   Son's of Jacob and Zilpah (Leah's handmaid)
7. Gad
8. Asher
   Son's of Jacob and Bilhah (Rachel's handmaid)
9. Dan
10. Napthali
    Son's of Jacob and Rachel (The favorite wife)
11. Joseph known as the dreamer; sold into slavery by his brothers; became a top officer in Egypt.
12. Benjamin; the youngest of them all; descendants known as the "Left-handed tribe";

*Joseph's sons received his territory because Joseph died before the division. They were: Ephraim and Manasseh.

The Judges of Israel
Years of Server

The judges were temporary and special deliverers, seat by God to deliver the Israelites from their Oppressors.

NOTE: The office of judge was so abused by Samuel's sons that the people demanded a king.

Judge's Name	*Years of Server*
1. Othniel	40 years to Mesopotamia
2. Ehud	18 years to Moab
3. Shangar	20 years to Jabin and Sisera
4. Deborah and Bauk	40 years
5. Gideon	40 years
6. Abimelech	3 years
7. Tola	23 years
8. Jair	22 years to Ammon 18 years
9. Jephthah	6 years
10. Ibzan	7 years
11. Elon	10 years
12. Abdon	8 years to the Philistines
13. Samson	20 years
14. Eli	40 years
15. Samuel	40 years

What Does the Bible Say About... (Holy Bible KJV)

Amen—Deuteronomy 27:15

> Nehemiah 8:1–6
> Psalms 89:52
> Romans 9:4,5
> 2 Corinthians 1:19,20
> Galatians 1:3–5
> 2 Peter 3:18

Abortion—Psalms 127:3

> Psalms 139:13–16
> Psalms 103:3–4
> 1 John 1:9

Aids and Homosexuality—1 Corinthians 6:9–11

> 2 Corinthians 5:17
> 2 Corinthians 4:17
> Romans 8:18–25

Alcoholics (KJV)—1 John 1:8,9

> Isaiah 26:3
> Proverbs 28:13
> Romans 11:1–2

Galatians 5:22,23
1 Corinthians 10:13

Anger—Proverbs 15:1

Proverbs 29:11
Ephesians 4:22–24
Colossians 3:8
James 1:19–20

Cults—Jude 20–23

Mark 14:38
1 John 4:1–3
2 Timothy 3:13–15
Colossians 1:17 and Colossians 1:15–16

Habits—Ephesians 2:10

Philippians 2:13–15
James 4:7–8
Romans 8:37
Romans 6:11–14

Pornography—Romans 8:6

Galatians 5:17
Romans 6:12
1 Corinthians 6:18
Romans 8:13
James 1:15

Satan—Ezekiel 28:15

John 8:44
Matthew 25:41

2 Corinthians 11:14
2Corinthians 4:4
1Peter 5:8–10

Divorce—Matthew 19:9

1Corinthians 7:15
Malachi 2:15,16
Matthew 18:21–22
1Corinthians 7:3–4
Philippians 2:3–5
1 Peter 3:7

Dreams and Visions—Genesis 15:1–5

Genesis 28:10–19
Acts 16:7–10
Matthew 13:55
Mark 6:3
Habakkuk 2:2,3

Fasting—Deuteronomy 9:9-18–21

2 Samuel 12:15–23
Ezra 8:21–23
Isaiah 58:1–14
Luke 18:10–14
Acts 13:1–3
Acts 14:21–23

Fruits of the Spirit (NIV)—Matthew 7:16

Galatians 5:22,23

Gifts of the Spirit—Ephesians 4:11,12

1 Corinthians 12:8–11

Jesus's Disciples (12 Origin) (KJV)

1. Andrew
   From Bethsaida; Simon Peter's brother, fisherman, he identified the boy with the five loaves of bread and the two fishes, he brought Simon Peter to Jesus.

2. Peter
   The Greek name for "Rock" also called Cephas. His name was Simon until Jesus gave him the name "Peter." (Mark 3:16) Peter was one of the three closest to Jesus. He denied Christ during the time of the crucifixion, but became a dynamic leader of the early church.

3. Phillip
   From Bethsaida; brought his brother Nathaniel to Jesus; helped with the feeding of the five thousand; brought Gentiles to Jesus.

4. Nathaniel
   A Canaanite; he is noted for his question, "Can any good come out of Nazareth?" One of the first disciples; identified as the Apostle Bartholomew.

5. Simon
   A Canaanite (The Zealot)

6. Thaddaeus
   Called Lebbaeus otherwise called Judas (son of James).

7. Thomas
   Called Didymus; often referred to as "Doubting Thomas."

8. Matthew
   Tax collector from Capernaum; otherwise known as Levi.

9. Judas Iscariot
   Notorious for betraying Jesus; prompted by Satan and greed; committed suicide.

10. James, Son of Zebedee
    The first disciple to be martyred; fisherman nicknamed "Son of Thunder"; one of the three closest to Jesus.

11. John, Son of Zebedee
    Nicknamed "Son of Thunder," fisherman; one of the trio closest to Jesus; younger brother of James.

12. Judas, Son of James
    Also known as Thaddaeus.

How Many?

1. Abraham's sons?
2. Number of the Hebrew boys?
3. The books in the Old Testament?
4. Phase 1 number of days in the wilderness?
5. Abraham's age when Isaac was born?
6. Number of elders in the New Heaven?
7. The tribes of Israel?
8. The Disciples?
9. The Books in the New Testament?
10. Noah's age when he built the Ark?
11. Number of sons of Noah?
12. Number wives of King Solomon?
13. Number of plagues of Egypt?
14. How many chapters in the book of Psalms?
15. Numbers of daughters of Jacob?
16. Number of times Jesus said forgive?
17. Longest chapter in Psalms?
18. How many days to the Pentecost?
19. How many thieves on the cross at Calvary?
20. Number of women at the tomb of Jesus?
21. Number of sons of Adam and Eve in the garden?
22. Number of years Solomon built the temple?
23. Number of years the Israelites were captives in Egypt?
24. Number of days of rain before the great flood?
25. Number days to build Noah's ark?
26. Number of Gospels in the New Testament?
27. Number of brothers of Jesus?
28. Number of years the Israelites spent in Babylon?

29. Number of sons of Eli?
30. Number of people in Noah's Ark?
31. Number of "I am's" in the book of John?
32. Number of days of Creation?
33. Numbers of Beatitudes?
34. Number of Judges of Israel?
35. Number of windows in the Ark?
36. Number of doors in the Ark?
37. Number of major Prophets?
38. Number of days of Jonah in the belly of the fish?
39. Number of pieces of silver—Judas?
40. Number of Solomon's concubines?
41. Number of minor Prophets?
42. Number of "woe" warnings of Jesus to the Pharisees?

Isaiah 40:8

> "The grass withereth, the flower fadeth, but the word of our GOD shall stand forever."

Romans 15:4

> "For whatsoever things were written aforetime were written for our learning, that we through patience and comfort of the scriptures might have hope."

Thanks...

Gratitude, appreciation, love, and those words that have the same meaning.

To my two sons, Wesley K. Chapman and Family and David L. Chapman and family for their love and support.

Betty Burgess my greatest friend, LaNika Fenty for her clerical and constructive support, my good-good friend Yvonne Patterson (See Exhibit #2) from Buffalo, New York, and Catherine Mann from North Carolina, thank you both for your love, support, and phenomenal encouragement. Ada Suarez, family members in Georgia and Florida, my adult Sunday School class, and my entire Phillips Metropolitan CME church family.

Also the Late Sr. Bishop Thomas Lanier Hoyt, Jr. and family, and Bishop James B. Walker and Mrs. Delois Walker as mentioned and my own Pastors: Rev. Paul D. Everett and Co-Pastor First Lady Dr. Valerie T. Everett

Special Thanks to:

My grandchildren: Jamani, Dayna, Amber, and Wesley C. for special support and attention. My daughter-in-law, Shyrlene with editing and clerical assistance.

Benedictions

1. Numbers 6:24–27 (KJV)
   The Lord speaks to Aaron
   The LORD bless thee, and keep thee…

2. Romans 16:25
   Now to Him that is of power…

3. 1 Corinthians 16:13
   16:23
   Watch ye, stand fast in the faith…

4. 2 Corinthians 13:11–14
   Finally, Brethren, farewell…

5. Galatians 6:18
   Brethren, the grace of our LORD…

6. Ephesians 6:23,24
   Peace be to the Brethren…

7. Philippians 4:23
   The Grace of our LORD…

8. Thessalonians 5:28
   The grace of our LORD…

9. Thessalonians 3:16
   Now the LORD of peace...

10. 2 Timothy 4:22
    The LORD JESUS CHRIST...

LET THERE BE LIGHT

Lillian in the post office days

The street Lillian grew up on

(L-R) Lillian's sons, David and Wesley, at a young age

David and Wesley

Phillips Metropolitan Church in Hartford, Connecticut

(L-R) Lillian's sister Arlene, mother Elnora, Aunt Gladys, and Lillian holding granddaughter Jazmyn

Phillips Metropolitan Church Family

(L-R) Bishop Hoyt (deceased), Pastor Green, Bishop Walker, and Presiding Elder Belcher.

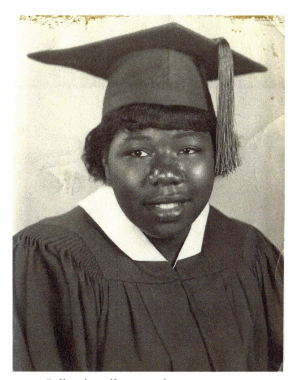

Lillian's college graduation picture

Lillian as a young girl in Georgia with sister and cousins

Lillian's high school graduation picture

Lillian all dressed for church

LET THERE BE LIGHT

Lillian and church members

Lillian (far right) with mom and dad.

Lillian with sister Arlene

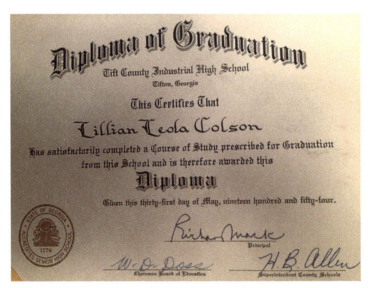

Lillian's high school diploma

Lillian with her sons David and Wesley at her appreciation dinner

Phillips Metropolitan Church Choir

Post Office in Bloomfield, CT where Lillian L. Graham was Postmaster

Lillian being honored at a Post Office event

Working – Post Office days

Lillian being sworn in as Postmaster of the Bloomfield Post Office

Left to right – Great Aunt Willie Mae McClinton, Sister Arlene, Lillian, and cousin Francis

Lillian in her youth

Lillian in her youth

Lillian in her youth

About the Author

Born in Adel Georgia, lived with my great-grandmother until age eight. Born to Mary Elnora Clowers Mays and McKinley Mays. In the year 1945, I was brought to Tifton, Georgia, to live with adopted parents Minnie Lee Lilley Colson and Norman Lee Colson.

EDUCATION:

>Attended Cook County School from (1st through fourth grade).
>1945–1954: Attended Tift County Industrial School in Tifton, Georgia
>1954–1957: Attended Spelman College in Atlanta, Georgia

WORK EXPERIENCE:

>1957–1965: Full-time employment with Connecticut General Life Insurance Company (known as Cigna)
>1965–1993: Full time employment with the United States Post Office Distribution Clerk;
>Promoted to Women's Program Coordinator; afterward to Equal Employment Opportunity Specialist; then to Postmaster Bloomfield, Connecticut
>Retired September 1993

CHRISTIAN EXPERIENCE:

>Baptized at the age of six at the Friendship Baptist Church Adel, Georgia

Joined Allen Temple African Methodist Episcopal Church-Tifton, Georgia (age eight).

1957: Became a member of the Phillips Metropolitan Christian Methodist Episcopal Church—Hartford, Connecticut

LOCAL CHURCH:

- President of the Gospel Chorus (1960–2000)
- Director Christian Education—55 years. (Resigned 2013)
- Trustee—20 years (Resigned 2008)
- Sunday School Teacher (1960–present)
- One Church/One School Coordinator (presently)

DISTRICT OFFICES (New York/New England):

- Director, Christian Education—5 years
- Director Youth Activities—5 years

ANNUAL CONFERENCE OFFICE - New York/Washington:

- Youth Ministry Director - New York-Washington-Virginia Region
- Director, Youth Activities, 1995–2000

NATIONAL LEVEL:

- Wrote handbook for Chaperones
- Chaperoned 15 + Youth to the Youth and Young Adult Conferences.
- Saint Louis Missouri, New Orleans Louisiana, Louisville Kentucky, Greensboro, North Carolina (2), Birmingham Alabama, Orlando, Florida (3).

FAMILY:

- Mother of two sons (Wesley and David)
- Ten grandchildren and one great granddaughter:

Ashley, Wesley, Jazmyn, Dayna, Jamani, Amber, Christopher, Destiney, Maya, Destinee and Micaylah.

God children: Shirley Thompson Ellison, Jeanette Carson, Byron Bobb, James Brown (not the famous singer), Kenneth and Domonique Brown.

"Blessings Called by my Name: People - Places -Venues"

People

During my studies at Spellman College, Rev. Martin Luther King, Sr. was chaplain and he conducted weekly vesper services. Rev. Martin Luther King, Jr. visited whenever he was home from college (before he became the great civil rights leader). I had a nexus with him since I was from Hartford, CT and he had done summer work in Windsor, CT (Hartford outskirt).

Being an English major, I took poetry writing courses under the famous Poet – Dr. Robert Lee Frost

Places visited – Vacation, Church and Occupational Travel

I visited 30 of the 50 United States of America, Canada, The Noah Webster, The Mark Twain House (Connecticut), the Statue of Liberty, Empire State Building, China Town, Coney Island (New York), the Hoover Dam (Nevada), Arizona Desert, Colorado River, Indian Reservation (Hollywood, CA and Maine), Beverly Hills, CA, Home of Madam C.J. Walker (Virginia), Disney World (Florida), Graceland (Tennessee), Glass Bottom Boat (Florida), The Fountain of Youth (Florida), Santa Land (Vermont), Santa Village (Maine), and I traveled to three Islands and cruised around the Kennedy Compound (Massachusetts).

Venues

I was appointed a member of a three- party team detailed to the United States Capitol (Washington, DC) to prepare a study on the feasibility of providing around the clock care to employees of the USPS. I was an audience member of a TV talk show (California).

Another accomplishment that I might mention is a group of young people whom I called "My Conference Kids". This is a group of young people who are members of the Christian Methodist Episcopal Church throughout the Northeast region. This includes Virginia through Massachusetts, Northeast USA. I was a conference elected officer in the young people's department and mentored the young people for several years. All I can hear about this group is good. They are adults now and some are preachers, teachers, airline workers, in the medical field, workers in real estate, and other professional fields. I have even heard that one young man is a cook in the nations White House. Others I have heard are proud parents of college students and college grads. I feel very proud and rewarded to say these things. Any bragging I do is about the love, support and enabling of my Lord and Savior Jesus Christ. God be the glory.

Twelve years ago, I lost my sight and part of my hearing. I am a diabetic, I have congestive heart failure, low blood pressure, I am on oxygen daily and I am a renal dialysis patient. I do not want any pity and I have no desire to question God, we live in a sinful world and sometimes things happen. I was able to see and do many things before I lost my vision, and still do what I can to enlarge God's Kingdom. Through it all God has been the light of my life. There have been some dark days and some dreary days, but I do know beyond the clouds the sun is always shining. What I'm saying is whatever is in God's will for me is also my will. I thank God for allowing me to watch my two sons grow into strong men and I'm so thankful for my ten grandchildren and great-granddaughter as they mature and begin on their journey in life.

Lillian passed away November 2, 2017.

Last picture taken of Lillian before her death

CPSIA information can be obtained
at www.ICGtesting.com
Printed in the USA
BVHW020652201220
596119BV00016B/223